Creative Techniques for
Photographing Children

VIK ORENSTEIN

WRITER'S DIGEST BOOKS

Cincinnati, Ohio

Photographer/writer Vik Orenstein owns and operates Kidshooters—a nationally recognized studio specializing in hand-colored child portraits. Vik shares her expertise in photographing kids on television talk shows and in national magazines. Her first book, *How to Break Into Modeling*, was published by Writer's Digest Books in 1987.

Creative Techniques for Photographing Children. Copyright © 1993 by Vik Orenstein. Photographs copyright © 1993 by Vik Orenstein. Printed and bound in Hong Kong. All rights reserved. No part of this book may be reproduced in any form or by any electronic or mechanical means including information storage and retrieval systems without permission in writing from the publisher, except by a reviewer, who may quote brief passages in a review. Published by Writer's Digest Books, an imprint of F&W Publications, Inc., 1507 Dana Avenue, Cincinnati, Ohio 45207; 1-800-289-0963. First edition.

97 96   5 4 3

Library of Congress Cataloging-in-Publication Data

Orenstein, Vik.
    Creative techniques for photographing children / by Vik Orenstein.
—1st ed.
        p.   cm.
    Includes index.
    ISBN 0-89879-543-5
    1. Photography of children. I. Title.
TR681.C5074   1993
778.9'25—dc20

92-22987
CIP

Edited by Diana Martin
Designed by Paul Neff

COURAGE IS SEEING THE WORLD
for what it is and loving it anyway. This book is dedicated in
celebration of Hannah Edgar, a courageous little girl.

I'D LIKE TO THANK THE FOLLOWING PEOPLE FOR THEIR HELP
ON THIS BOOK:

Erik Rusley, my husband and partner

Oscar Collier, my literary agent

William Brohaugh, my editor

Dale Wolf, my faithful and tireless nitpicker

Lee Stanford, for technical advice and encouragement

Lynn Schoenstedt, photo color artist and the
Queen of Orange

Rita Schoenstedt, photo color artist and the Queen Mother

Martha Edgar, photo color artist

Amira Stanford, for black-and-white printing and comic relief

The gang at Procolor, especially Eileen and John

Craig Gallagher, owner, Drop Everything

Julie Dornisch, owner, Simply Splendid

Cynthia Gerdes, owner, Creative Kid Stuff

Tia McNeil, owner, Belini

Michael Earhart, for helping to clear the way

THE KIDS WHO APPEAR IN THE BOOK:

Ariane Ackerberg	Brynne Edgar	Robin Jones	Gavie McNeil	Tony Sonifer
Sam Ackerberg	Carly Eve Ettinger	Ryan Kellogg	Alexander Buhler Oser	Anthony Stanford
Hannah Lisa Anderson	Brett Cole Fingerhut	Andrew Lee Kitzenberg	Caroline Elisabeth	Ben Stein
Ben Barghini	Abby Mackenzie Fink	Celine Marie	Owens	Brooke Stein
Caroline Berg	Madlyn Friedenfeld	Kitzenberg	Cole Zhores Paiement	Carly Stein
Peter Berg	Maren Knepper Frisell	David Alan Kitzenberg	Ashley Peck	Lauren Stein
Stuart Berg	Gabbie Fulmer	Simon Kohnstamm	Breanna Peck	Brett Striker
Eva Caroline Boehnke	Logan Fulmer	Sloane Kohnstamm	Chelsey Peck	Erin Striker
Krista Bolles	Lon Garelick	Kazuta Kuroki	Brian Pueschold	Matthew Davis Thiel
Lauren Bolles	James Gilchrist	Mia Kuroki	Michael Pueschold	Travis Jordan Thiel
Lindsay Bolles	Sam Graber	Blakey Hartnett Larsen	Natalia Pueschold	Chase Turner
Whitney Bolles	Spencer Graber	Peter Hartnett Larsen	Ashley Ring	Lark Turner
Alexa Camarena	Zachary Graber	Amanda Lee	Mishawn Ring	Melley Turner
Talia Camarena	Jerry Graunke	Mercedes Lee	Andrea Rutchik	Mills Turner
Lauren Carisch	Madeline Graunke	Lillian O'Brien Lelich	Max Rutchik	Katie Veechi
Marisha	Omar Een Hajji	Rosemary O'Brien	Ronni Saxon	Tomecia C. Watson
Arianna	Soraya Een Hajji	Lelich	Samantha Shaller	Louise Winslow
Michael Jacob	Vanessa Brooke Hanley	Beth Masters	Stacey Shaller	Alexandra Wolf
Christensen	Ashley Heltne	Emily Masters	Alison Sipkins	Mia Wolf
Sonja Ann Christensen	Jessica Ann Hennes	Gerrid McMorrow	Nicole Sipkins	Danny Wozniak
Zachary Dorman-Jones	Justine Nicole Hennes	Freddie McNeil	Crystal Sonifer	Kevin Wozniak

THE ADULTS WHO APPEAR IN THE BOOK:

Michael Fink	Kazunori Kuroki	Tom Paiement	Abby Rutchik	Michelle Shaller
Patti Kelly	Ruth Kuroki	Brian Pueschold	Orrie Rutchik	Ellyn Stein
				Mike Striker

THE AMATEUR PHOTOGRAPHERS WHOSE WORK APPEARS:

Maret Hensick	Marnie Jones	Wendy Zueli

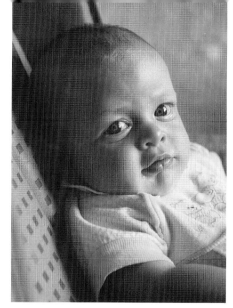

The mom who shot this portrait is a singer and musician by trade, but her artistic bent extends into photography as well.

Photo by Marnie Jones.

There are a million wonderful reasons for making photographs of children. Parents document their children's growth and development, and sometimes create portraits worthy of display as decorative objects. Professional photographers create commercial pieces and portraits of children for profit. A fine art photographer creates art pieces featuring children. A photojournalist captures the feeling and spirit of a single family, an entire culture, or even a moment in history in the faces of her child subjects.

My husband/partner Erik Rusley and I came by our specialty of child photography quite by accident after working in architectural and commercial areas. I started Kidshooters as *revenge* against grandma. (Sorry, Grandma Esther. I love you just the same.)

Grandma used to take my sister and me to have frequent formal portraits made when we were small. Whether the portrait was a photograph, a charcoal drawing or a silhouette cutting, the process always involved the cruel and unusual punishment of having our hair "fixed" and being forced into dresses with scratchy tulle skirts, twisted tights and pinching shoes, and—horrors!—being made to *sit still*. Then, in the mid '70s, when action shots became de rigueur in fashion magazines, I thought to myself, "Now that's the way kids should be photographed—running, leaping and laughing. And wearing their 'everyday' clothes."

For a full decade I railed to anyone who would listen about the sad state of children's portraiture, until I finally decided to be quiet and do something about it. The results have been outstanding. Our black-and-white and hand-colored portraits of children tripled the size of our business in the first year, and we're still growing. The Kidshooters arm of Rusley Design and Photography has earned us television appearances and articles and cover photos in national magazines.

More important than the financial rewards or the recognition we've received through Kidshooters are the kids we've come to know and love. We've met all kinds of kids: healthy and ill, of many ethnic backgrounds, pampered and poor, and many with special needs. Erik and I had minimal experience with children when we began Kidshooters and didn't know what to expect—Would sick children be sad? Would pampered ones be spoiled? Would the physically challenged be somehow different from the able-bodied? We have discovered that no matter what adversity kids face or privilege they enjoy, they have a strength of spirit many adults would envy. They all respond with delight to genuine warmth, respect and attention.

Everyone reading this book will have different reasons for their interest in child photography. But whatever your reasons or level of technical expertise, the fascination with childhood's abundant beauty, grace and wonder unites.

A NOTE TO THE PARENT/ AMATEUR PHOTOGRAPHER You may not be a professional, but you have the two things that make for a superb children's photographer. Coincidentally, they are the same two things that make for a superb criminal suspect: opportunity and motive.

You spend lots of time with your kids. They already know and love you; you don't have to earn their trust. You're privy to those real-life moments that make great photos. If you pull out your camera often, tinker with it, and shoot casually while your children are engaged in everyday play instead of hauling it out just for birthday and Christmas "lineups" (*Now say cheese*), they will accept your photographic endeavors and you will be rewarded with success. Happily, you're lacking only two things that the professional photographer has: a studio and an awareness of equipment, materials and techniques.

This book will help you learn the technical and creative skills that will help you

This picture was taken by a mom who learned how to shoot and print her own beautiful, professional-looking portraits of her daughter in a few photography classes through community education programs.

Photo by Wendy Zeuli.

take great shots of your kids. Then when those magic moments arise, you won't wonder which lens to use, fumble for the wrong roll of film, or keep your fingers crossed that you have the right light. And while it's true that you don't have the control a studio provides, this book will help you use available light and locations like a pro. You'll create candid pictures that are every bit as precious, and perhaps more personal and intimate, than studio shots.

Don't assume that you need thousands of dollars of equipment to take fantastic photos. In my studio, I have at my disposal enough types of artificial light sources to shoot a different lighting look each day for a year. But my favorite way to shoot is to use natural window light and two cardboard reflectors. I have heard it said (in reference to mathematics) that simplicity is elegance. I believe this is also true in photography. The beautiful portraits that illustrate this introduction were shot by parent/amateur photographers.

A NOTE TO PROFESSIONAL PHOTOGRAPHERS

There is a greater demand now for child photographers than ever before. The popularity of portraits as art and decorative objects, especially black-and-white photos, has resurged. Two-career families with children (and discretionary income) have the sophistication to look beyond photo mills and conventional portrait studios and to demand and recognize the value of unique and beautiful work.

In the commercial world, children are being used in ads selling products totally unrelated to diapers, toys or kids' clothes. Think of the babies featured in ads and television spots for Michelin tires. Stock photo agencies have a greater need for work featuring children as well.

And, of course, there always have been, and always will be, fine art and journalistic photographers focusing their attentions on children. No matter what your area of photographic specialty, you can increase your business by learning to put your knowledge and creative techniques to work with children.

Whether you're a serious amateur photographer preserving moments of your children's lives or a professional photographer shooting kids for commercial, portrait, fine art or journalistic applications, I hope this book will help you in celebrating the beauty and nature of children.

—Vik Orenstein

Portraits made in the studio needn't be formal — this studio shot has the spontaneity of a candid.

Strobes; studio; Nikon 8008; Nikkor 35-105mm zoom AF lens; Kodak Plus-X 100 (b&w professional film).

5

An artist of any medium can choose no better subject than a child. Endlessly energetic, constantly changing, guileless, naturally beautiful — children make eternally intriguing, charming, exciting subjects. By portraying a child, you break open in the viewer a stronghold of feelings, memories and experiences, for we all have been children. An artfully and thoughtfully executed photograph of a child can awaken in the viewer feelings of security and vulnerability, joy and grief, playfulness and solemnity, all of an intensity that we may have long forgotten we're capable of. Children in and of themselves are works of art.

THE PERFECT SUBJECT

When I talk about my work as a photographer, I always say that I make pictures, not take pictures. A painter doesn't "take" a painting, and a sculptor doesn't "take" a sculpture. "Taking a picture" implies that the image is out there waiting to be picked, like a flower. In fact, when a photographer points a camera at a subject, she is not simply recording the image, she is interpreting it, and the tens of choices she makes — film type, f-stop, exposure, lens, format, manipulation of light, perspective, interaction with the subject, framing, to name just a few — make the finished picture uniquely her own. If you think you are merely "taking a picture," you may be seriously limiting yourself. While there is only one way to take a picture, there are millions of ways to *make* a picture.

THE PHOTOGRAPHIC ATTITUDE

The best photographers use their art to interpret and comment on our world. Photography is not simply a tool of documentation. While it *might be* possible to record an image photographically that seems to look exactly as the subject appeared to the naked eye at the moment it was made — an image, in other words, that seems real — the best photographs are not so literal; they are enhanced through the eyes of the photographer to evoke moods and emotions.

Think about how we as human beings see an image. Only once do we see a moment as it actually happened. Then we see it again many times as we replay it in our memories, colored by our personal experiences, biases and the passage of time. Who is to say that the way the images appear to us in memory are inferior to "the

*Creative
Techniques for
Photographing
Children*

**Kids make great subjects even when they are
showing off.**

Strobes; studio; Nikon 8008; Nikkor 35-105mm zoom AF lens;
Fuji Velvia 50 (professional film).

real thing"? When I make pictures, I try to make them feel the way memories feel—
soft, impressionistic and full of emotional significance.

I love to engage in heated discussions with other photographers about what types
of film are best for photographing people, and kids in particular. A good friend of
mine champions Ektachrome because, he says, "It produces skin tones that look
more real." My response to him is: "I don't want my pictures to look real. I want them
to *feel* real."

Once you've realized that making pictures *is* an art, a whole new realm of artistic
and interpretive freedom opens up to you. And what subject befits an artist better
than a child?

**ARTISTIC
FREEDOM**

Of course, the ultimate use of the photograph will affect the amount of artistic freedom you exercise. If you're shooting for your own use and enjoyment, the sky's the
limit. But if you're shooting for a client (portrait, commercial, stock or gallery), you
may have more restrictions.

Ask yourself before you shoot, "Why am I making this picture? For the family
photo album? To create a portrait to hang on my wall? To sell a product? To sell as an
art piece? To record a moment of history?"

Regardless of the intended use, all great photographs of kids stand on their own
outside of any context: They all begin as *art portraits*.

**WHAT IS AN ART
PORTRAIT?**

To begin to define what an art portrait is, let's look at the two words: art and portrait.
According to *Webster's New Collegiate Dictionary*:

Art: *the conscious use of skill and creative imagination especially in the
production of aesthetic objects.*

Portrait: *a pictorial representation of a person usually showing his face.*

Combining these definitions gives us, roughly, "a pictorial representation of a person
made with the conscious use of skill and creative imagination." To this I presume to
add several criteria of my own. To be successful as an art portrait, the work should
also:

• **Be decorative.** Most direct color, formal portraits do not stand on their own
as decorative objects. People tend to purchase these in 5 × 7 and 8 × 10 prints to set
on a shelf or hang on "the photo wall" in a hallway, to be replaced by the next year's

photo. In contrast, an art portrait can be displayed any place one would normally hang other "art," frequently in places of high visibility: over mantels, in entries and great rooms. The work remains even when updated portraits are added to the home as the child matures.

- **Show your creative intent.** If you make a photograph with the intent to surpass mere documentation and create artwork that expresses your subject's true essence, you will probably succeed. Conversely, if you make the photo intending only to create a functional representation of your subject (or in the case of a professional photographer, a product for which your client will pay a lot of money), you may fail in achieving either an artistic statement or a marketable portrait.

- **Incorporate skill and emotion.** While a work must be well crafted to succeed, skill alone is not enough to satisfy the definition of art. In addition to being skillfully executed, the work should evoke some emotion in the viewer.

- **Capture the essence of your subject.** An art portrait should, as I mentioned before, go beyond simple documentation of the subject's physical appearance. *Personality*—those traits, habits and expressions that make each of us unique—should be evoked, and the social façade should be penetrated. (Yes, even babies have a social facade.) While this quality of personality may seem intangible, I think we all have an instinctive awareness of what gestures and expressions are genuine. I present clients

**Technique can help you capture the spirit of a child.
Here I used a hard side light to emphasize the theatrical
feeling of the boy's gestures and displayed three shots
together to show his fantastic range of expression.**

Strobes; studio; Nikon 8008; Nikkor 35-105mm AF lens; Kodak
Plus-X 100 (b&w professional film).

with proof sheets on which I've marked the shots I personally find most successful, and I'm frequently rewarded with comments such as, "Oh, yes, that's *really* him!" or, "Yes, you've captured his *natural* look." Successful portraits needn't be all smiles, but may represent many different moods.

• **Complement your subject.** Your use of applied or direct (i.e., natural) color, technique, setting, props and other photographic elements ideally will enhance your representation of your subjects rather than diminish or compete with them.

PHOTOGRAPHIC GENRES

Now, if you approach every picture you make of a child as an art portrait, you will find that it can cross over into several, if not all, of the common photographic genres.

• Candids refer to any shots that are taken of kids in their own environment, busy at play, not performing for the camera. Some people also call candids "informal portraits." Candids may be made by amateurs or professionals.

• Studio portraits are made by professional photographers in the controlled studio environment, usually commissioned by the children's parents for their personal use.

• Environmental portraits are made by professional photographers outside of the studio. Popular locations for environmental portraits are wooded areas or the child's own home or yard.

- Commercial photographs are made by photographers who specialize in advertising work.

- Stock photos are made by professional photographers and photojournalists but are sold by stock agencies to commercial and industrial clients for innumerable uses. The same photo can be resold to many different clients worldwide. These photos are sometimes made for the express purpose of being sold as stock; other times they are photos that were originally made for personal, commercial or journalistic purposes. Pictures of children are in good demand by stock agencies.

- Journalistic photos tell stories about kids in our world today. The photojournalists who make them work freelance, on self-assignment, frequently with the aid of grants, and on assignment for newspapers and magazines.

- Decorative art photographs are created by professional photographers and published by poster companies for hanging in residences and offices. A good percentage of decorative art features children, especially black-and-white and hand-colored photos.

- Fine art photography, including some work featuring children, is enjoying new popularity. Limited editions of black-and-white prints, and even direct-color photos made by professional photographers are sold by art and frame galleries.

I focus most of my work on black-and-white and hand-colored techniques, because these give me almost total artistic control. I try to portray, not miniature adults, but natural kids, just being themselves.

Strobes; studio; Nikon FE2; Nikkor 35-105mm zoom AF lens; Kodak Plus-X 100 (b&w professional film).

At least two people are captured in every photo: the subject and the photographer. No matter how anonymous the photographer tries to be, her personal style appears in every photo. Each of us has a personal style that is comprised of the following elements:

• Special vision—our way of seeing, colored by experiences, philosophy and attitudes.

• Feelings about ourselves, children, ourselves as children, the universal experience of childhood and our own personal childhoods.

• Reasons for making pictures of children: to convey a message, for display as an art piece, for our personal use or as a way of celebrating childhood.

• The audience for whom we make the picture: the subject, a commercial client, the subject's parent(s), a stock agency or simply for ourselves.

• Strengths and weaknesses—personal, technical and artistic—are elements of personal style.

• Knowledge of techniques that allow us to creatively use tools and materials (such as lighting, film types and props) to create images.

Do you need good technique to express your vision, or do you need a vision before you can explore and apply various techniques and materials? To facilitate either preference, this book is divided into three sections that you can read in any order. Whether you develop your technique or your style first is your decision.

HOW TO DEVELOP YOUR STYLE

Developing your style is like bodybuilding: You already have muscles, but you want to make them bigger or more defined. You already have a personal style, but you want to make it bolder, more distinct. Just as there are muscle-building exercises, so are there style-building exercises:

1. **Follow your bliss.** Shoot kids the way you love to see them. Do you like the grace and energy of childhood? Make action pictures of kids running, jumping and dancing. Do you want to show the tender, vulnerable side of children? Shoot candids of kids in pensive moods.

2. **Personalize your photographs.** Interpret, don't just record your subjects.

Communicate your personal feelings about the kids in your pictures and the pictures themselves.

3. **Enjoy the process.** We all enjoy having made a beautiful picture. But we should also enjoy the process of making the picture. Everything from the concept (who, what, where, why and how to make a picture) to the actual execution (interacting with the child, metering the light, even clicking the shutter) should intrigue and excite you. If it does, it will come across in your work and enhance your style.

4. **Let wrong be right.** Rather than searching for the "correct" exposure, the "correct" film type or the "correct" lens, you can explore doing things "incorrectly." Perhaps overexposing a certain image will make it beautifully ethereal; underexposing another may give it a rich, moody quality; using a wide-angle lens might transmit a feeling of isolation or expansiveness; shooting in tungsten light with daylight film may create a warm feeling. Many contemporary photographers have forged wildly successful careers by making pictures "the wrong way." Chip Simmons, a commercial photographer, is best known for his pictures made with a fish-eye lens and colored gels. Out of focus, mixed light sources, chrome film processed with negative film chemistry, and negative film processed with chrome chemistry—this is just a start of the many "wrong" possibilities.

5. **Experiment.** Give yourself hands-on experience with every possible technique, piece of equipment and material you can find. If you like the results, great. If you don't, throw the shots out. You can't possibly know what a given film type, technique or process can do until you try it. When you come across a medium that helps you express your vision, refine it, master it, make it your own.

6. **Welcome failure.** You can't be innovative and try new techniques without failing once in a while. And it really is true that you learn more from your failures than you do from your successes. From my own experience, I know that if I had only attempted photographic techniques that were guaranteed to succeed, I would never have shot a single frame.

Be willing to fail, but be sure to leave yourself a safety net if you shoot professionally. When you try out a new technique or medium, use your own kids or friends of the family before offering it to clients. Present your experimentation to your subjects and their parents as a "photo test." Explain to them that you're trying out a new idea and if the results are good, you'll give them a complimentary print. That way no one will be overly surprised or disappointed if your attempts fall short.

7. **Let your style evolve.** While it's important to be aware of what you're trying to say in making your pictures and to realize that your personal style is shaping the

outcome of your shooting, it's also important not to overanalyze or overcontrol your approach. Indulge your joys and interests. Don't allow your style to remain static—the most successful photographers' styles evolve constantly. Just as the caterpillar forgot how to walk when asked which leg went first, so too can you lose your momentum temporarily if you think too much about what you're doing.

Especially if you're new at photography, or new in the area of children's photography, you might not yet be fully expressing your personal style. Rest assured; it will emerge through experience.

How my style evolved. As I mentioned in the introduction, my personal style of photographing children springs in part from my averse reaction to the way photos of me in my childhood were made. I was motivated to make pictures of kids as both a means of celebrating children and of self-expression.

I decided to make portraits, in particular, because I think the photo mill and traditional methods of portraiture not only fail to portray their subjects, but are also artless and nonarchival. So I made it my personal quest to make pictures of kids that portrayed their spirit and personalities, that would be worthy of display as art and decorative pieces, and would be archivally preserved, so they could be enjoyed by my subjects' children in decades to come. This *vision*, these *feelings*, these *reasons*, and this *message* all were the basis from which my style began to emerge.

From there I experimented with the different photographic mediums, and quickly settled on black-and-white and hand-colored pictures. I found that these mediums helped me meet several of my goals: black and white and applied color are classic, timeless techniques, which, when executed with archival materials, will last indefinitely. Since I did my own black-and-white printing, these mediums gave me almost total artistic control over every detail of the final pictures.

I set out to portray my impression of kids—real, moving, casually dressed, with runs in their stockings, crooked neckties, falling straps and messy hair—not the formally dressed and posed, perfectly still "miniature adults" in conventional portraits. My fascination with movement and the informal approach led me to concentrate on full-length rather that head shots.

Not happy relying on one shot to show a kid's entire range of expression, I presented my work in a series of three to nine shots, so that many moods, from pout to whimsy, could all work together to tell a story about the child.

Finally, my ultimate expression of movement came in my current specialty, what I call isolation collages. Avant-garde cropping and image juxtaposition exaggerates the child's movement to create a highly energized piece.

Part of my style involves presenting three or more shots together, to portray a range of expressions and movement. I call this an isolation collage—my own expression of a child's energy and movement.

Strobes; studio; Nikon FE2; Nikkor 35-105mm zoom AF lens; Kodak Plus-X (b&w professional film); printed on Agfa Portriga 118 matte paper; colored with Marshall photo oils and pencils, and artist's oils.

There is nothing new under the sun.

The art of photography has been around for a bazillion years. Every medium you can possibly conceive has been used by countless others before you. By the time new spins on old materials trickle down to the photography magazines, they've often been done to death by pros on both coasts. Given the limitations of the materials and mediums, the anatomical sameness of human subjects (one head, two eyes, two ears, a nose, a mouth), some might despair of ever making an original or creative picture.

WHAT MAKES A PICTURE CREATIVE?

Originality is the *personalized approach* that makes a creative picture. The simplest, most straightforward techniques and materials can create highly creative works when the photographer applies her unique way of seeing and puts herself into her pictures without holding back. And being unrestrained means *taking risks*. By nature, creativity itself is not risk-free. So to make an original, creative work means going into uncharted territory. Without the potential for failure, there is no originality.

Sometimes to be creative you have to make it up as you go. This can give you what some call the impostor syndrome—the fear that you'll be exposed as somehow not good enough or not knowing enough. You must value your talents and trust your ability.

Creativity is capitalizing on your mistakes. As the old saying goes, "A good photographer isn't someone who never makes mistakes. A good photographer is someone who can repeat his mistakes." Mistakes, or accidents, can become the basis for exciting and original new techniques. In the pursuit of originality, it's important to be undaunted by "being wrong."

Creativity uses both intuition and intent. Intuition: subconscious insight and understanding; and intent: conscious judgment and technical expertise working together to create successful photographs. Intuition gives pictures impact, while intent gives you the means to express your intuition.

This portrait, made in our studio for the subject's parents, could also cross over into other genres such as
decorative art, commercial and stock photography.

Strobes; studio; Nikon 8008; Nikkor 180/2.8 AF lens; Fuji
Velvia 50.

16

WHAT KEEPS A PICTURE FROM BEING CREATIVE?

Novelty in the use of materials, or unusual cropping and style don't make a picture creative, and perhaps more important, they don't make a picture good. Photographs that are avant-garde or different for the sake of being different may yield results that are self-conscious, overly precious or just simply weird. Secret formulas for processing, printing and lighting, and being the first and only one to use them won't make your work creative.

Perfection doesn't equal originality nor does it guarantee a great photograph. In fact, I'm not certain a perfect photograph even exists. Far worse, the quest for perfection can cause paralyzing fear, which I'm convinced has prevented uncountable original pictures from being made.

Working alone doesn't insure creativity. Having a collaborator—a commercial client, an art director, a photographic stylist or a portrait client—doesn't mean your input, or the ultimate product, will be any less original or successful than a work you create alone. In fact, my collaborations with commercial and portrait clients have resulted in some surprisingly original work. And many pictures that were created for commercial clients to sell a product actually stand on their own as great photographs.

Complaining about limitations won't make your pictures more creative, either. Imposed limitations, even ones that seem trivial and unreasonable (*Match this portrait to the colors in my sofa, please*), can sometimes result in highly original work. Think of other areas of art in which artificial limitations are embraced—if Shakespeare hadn't written within the strict form of iambic pentameter, we wouldn't have his sonnets.

BORROWING IDEAS AND TECHNIQUES

You (as a photographer, seasoned professional or amateur) can learn many new ideas and techniques to add to your creative repertoire from your peers. But where is the line between inspiration and imitation? When do we evolve from borrowing to stealing, or even copyright infringement of another photographer's work?

Use the work of other photographers, visual artists and even musicians and writers, as a jumping-off place to create your own original work. Dissect the work; determine what elements make it successful in your estimation and what elements are incidental to its success. Then elaborate on the *spirit* of the work, the medium or the technique, but not the work in its entirety, unless you're using it purely as a learning exercise. Never sell a literal re-creation of another's work to a client. And never try to pass off another's technique or invention as your own. Always acknowledge the sources for your inspiration, and you'll be less likely to be accused of imitation.

On the other hand, whether you share your own discoveries and techniques is up to you. In my experience, photographers who are confident in their abilities are most generous with their knowledge. Of course, when you share your techniques there is always the chance that someone will attempt a direct rip-off of your methods, and may even try to compete with you for clients in your own market. But technique alone doesn't make your work original and creative — it's also your personal vision, which is inimitable.

Composing head shots vertically focuses attention fully on the subject.

Available light; studio; Nikon 8008; Nikkor 180/2.8 zoom AF lens;
3M Scotch 1000 (chrome film).

Composition is the element of photography that seems to me to be the least considered. Many photographers seem to think a good composition is framing the child in the center of the shot without cutting off the head. But a good portrait—one that is well composed—includes not just framing but perspective, field and color. All of these elements should work together to create movement: a great composition makes the viewer's eye flow across the picture.

We tend to make horrible assumptions about composition. Amateur photographers assume that every subject is best shot horizontally; it rarely occurs to anyone to turn their camera sideways for a vertical shot; many assume that the subject belongs in the center of the frame; traditional portrait photographers are especially guilty of assuming that there should be lots and lots of empty space around the subject.

Shake your head and get rid of all those old *assumptions*. Here are some general rules for composition. But remember, rules are made to be broken!

1. Switch off your horizontal hold button.

Ninety percent of the time when you're shooting a human subject, your best format will be vertical. This holds true whether you're shooting full-body, midrange or head shots. Full-length shots have obvious strong vertical lines. The vertical lines of a head shot are less obvious, but looking at the photo of the boy (opposite), note that the line from the top of a human head to the collar bone is about three times as long as the line at the widest horizontal point running from ear to ear. You can even frame the child diagonally to emphasize line and movement.

2. You don't have to limit subject placement to the center of the picture.

In a formally balanced, traditional portrait, the appropriate treatment has the subject centered in the frame. However, formal balance is not as simple or as limiting as it sounds. There are many ways to frame (position your subject within the picture). For head shots, you can center the eyes or the head. With multiple subjects, you can center one subject or both. For three-quarter and full-body shots, you can center the subject's eyes, head or body. Again, as for multiple subjects in head shots, you can center just one or all of the subjects.

SIX RULES FOR GOOD FRAMING

You can add visual interest with diagonal framing. In the first shot, it gives this future businessman an air of busy-ness; of being "on-the-go." In the second shot, the slight diagonal framing emphasizes the tension created by the kids balancing on the railroad track.

Near right: Sunlight; outdoors; Nikon 8008; Nikkor 180/2.8 AF lens; Kodachrome 200 (professional film).

Far right: Sunlight; outdoors; Nikon 8008; Nikkor 180/2.8 AF lens; Fuji Velvia 50.

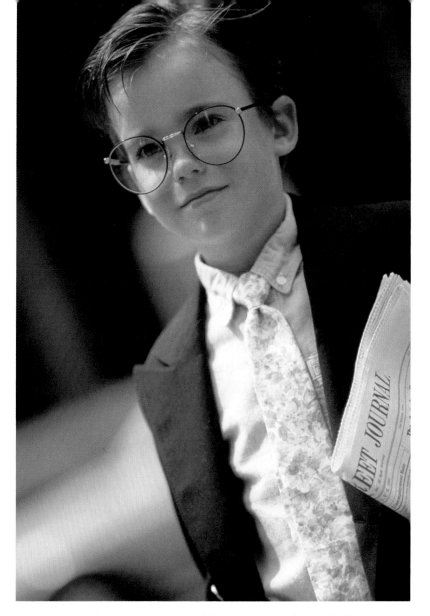

Some compositions can be made more exciting if the subject is framed off center (informal balance), which can create drama and tension. For example, if your subject is looking off out of the frame, you can place her off center to create a space for her to look into. And if several different shots are juxtaposed together in a series or collage, they may benefit from being composed with an eye toward informal balance to create or emphasize movement from picture to picture. These are just two choices of many. Let each subject's pose and the setting dictate whether you employ formal or informal balance in your composition.

3. Fill up the frame with the kid.

For most, the first impulse is to show too much of the subject's surroundings by shooting too wide. You don't need much background or foreground to evoke the mood of the setting. What you imply is as important as what you actually show. Notice how in the illustration on page 29, you know immediately that this boy is sitting on a fire truck, even though very little of the truck is actually in the frame.

You don't have to have a lot of space around the child—in fact, you don't even have to show the whole child. Head shots can be very successful with no space above the head, and even with part of the top of the head cropped off. Full-length shots generally need a little space above and below the subject, but think before you shoot. Do you really need the whole figure from head to toe, or would this be a better composition if it were shot tighter—say, head to midthigh, or even tighter?

One exception to the rule of filling the frame with the kid is if an object in the field becomes a compositional element that complements or balances the subject, such as in the illustration on page 30. In this case, you must frame the shot wider to include the object.

4. **The eyes have it.**

Generally—but not always—it's most desirable for the person viewing the photograph to be first drawn to the face, and especially to the eyes of the subject, because eyes are far and away our most expressive feature. This can be accomplished effectively in simple and complex compositions by employing formal and informal balance.

5. **Maintain only one center of interest.**

Even when there is more than one subject—though the composition becomes more complex—you should still only have one center of interest. Generally, to maintain the flow of your composition, the subjects should be touching one another or overlapping in some way. When photographing multiple subjects in head shots, the

I could have framed this shot with the boy's head or
eyes centered; I centered his eyes because it emphasizes them more.

Creating
Great
Compositions

Tungsten theatrical lights; studio; Nikon 8008; Nikkor 180/2.8 AF
lens; Fujichrome 400 (professional film).

heads should be close together and the bodies overlapping, as well. It's not always
natural for people to position themselves so close together, but some ways to solve
this problem are discussed in more length in chapter 12.

6. **Make shapes within your composition.**

Once I brought a five-year-old French girl into the darkroom with me to show her
how a print was made. I was working on an isolation collage that involved a lot of
avant-garde cropping. "What are you doing? Why do you make only parts of the
picture?" she asked. I was struggling to figure out how to explain composition to her
in words that would overcome our language barrier, when suddenly she said, "Oh, I
see, you are making shapes!" Voilà!

Here are some simple guidelines for making shapes of people in pictures:
• Keep the eyes of the subject in the upper third of the frame.
• Don't crop off limbs at the joints or the person will look like an amputee.
• To balance a shot that is cropped tightly below the subject, crop it tightly from
the top, and vice versa.
• If you shoot a child full-body, leave more space above the head than below the
feet to avoid the feeling that your subject is floating or that her head is crowded.

These rules may seem like a lot to remember in the heat of photographing an
active subject, but after a while it will become second nature, and you will automatically
compose your photos.

Field is the foreground, middle ground and background of a photograph. If you
pretend that the picture is three dimensional and turn it sideways, you can imagine
these spatial areas. By visualizing your subject's surroundings in three dimensions
you can more effectively create compositions that draw the eye to your center of
interest—the child. Here are some rules for using field in your compositions:

**FOUR RULES
FOR WORKING
WITH FIELDS**

1. **Use objects in the foreground.**

Putting objects in the foreground can frame the shot, add depth and visual interest, and lead the viewer's eye to the subject. This is a trick of the trade for architectural
photographers, who have been known to carry their own tree branches to dangle in
front of the camera, just in case the flora around their subject doesn't suffice. On
location, it's relatively easy to find objects that lend themselves naturally to use in the
foreground: toys, foliage, curtains, architectural elements, and even other people. But
in the studio, take special care that anything you put in the foreground doesn't look
too contrived.

In the first shot, the older boy is framed in the center, and his brother is off center; in the second shot, both subjects are centered.

Strobes; studio; Nikon 8008; Nikkor 35-105mm zoom AF lens; Fuji Velvia 50.

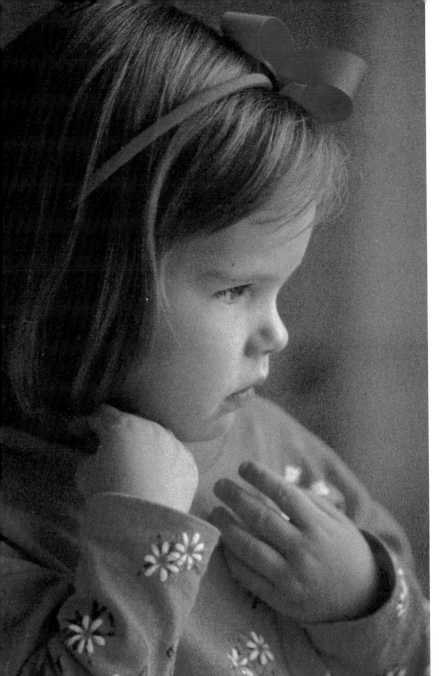

When your subject is looking out of the frame, give her some space to look into.

Available light; studio; Nikon 8008; Nikkor 180/2.8 AF lens; 3M Scotch (chrome film), push processed 1 stop.

2. Have only one center of interest in the middle ground.

The middle ground is where your subject is. Objects on the same plane as your subject are also in the middle ground. Since these objects pull attention away from the child, select them with care. If possible, position them in such a way that they are in contact with the subject and are thus a part of the center of interest of the photograph.

3. Keep the background simple and uncluttered.

Focus attention on the child. If I shoot on location and the surroundings are a key part of the picture, the trick is to lift the subject off the background by de-emphasizing, not eliminating, it. You can do this by shooting with a shallow depth of field, which means that the subject remains in focus as well as anything on the same plane (the middle ground), while anything in front of or behind the subject (the foreground and background) is slightly out of focus. Shallow depth of field is achieved by shooting at

**Fill up the frame with the kid(s)! You don't need a lot
of background or empty space.**

Strobe; studio; Nikon 8008; Nikkor 180/2.8 AF lens; Tiffen #1 soft
focus filter; Fuji Velvia 50.

a wide open f-stop with most lenses, or by shooting with a long (135 to 180mm) lens.
(More on lenses in chapter 8.)

4. **Position the horizon line above or below the middle of the shot and
the center of interest.**

If the horizon line is exactly centered, or, for instance, it bisects the subject's eyes,
it will distract and lead the eye out of the photo, instead of into it.

Some people photograph from their own eye level all the time. This is a big mistake, **FIVE RULES OF**
because the perspective you choose can greatly influence the mood, hence, the entire **PERSPECTIVE**
message of the picture. This is never more true than when the subject is a child. The
perspective of a photograph sends us messages both consciously and subconsciously,
and shapes our feelings about the subject. Shooting from different perspectives can
also help a photographer manipulate his field to the best advantage.

Implication is as important as actuality in your pictures. In this portrait the whole fire truck is implied by just the small area you see around the boy.

Open shade; outdoors; Nikon 8008; Nikkor 180/2.8 AF lens; Fuji Reala 100 (professional film).

1. **Shoot looking down at the child to enhance an air of innocence or vulnerability.**

Shooting down foreshortens your subject, making the child seem even smaller than he really is. It also shows more of the top of the head, making it necessary in head shots to crop more off the crown to make the child's eyes appear in the upper third of the frame.

2. **Shoot at the child's level to see eye to eye.**

Being on the same level lets the viewer identify with the child—literally seeing things "on his level."

3. **Shoot looking up at the child to emphasize accomplishment.**

Putting the child up on a higher level than the camera lends him an air of pride and competence.

4. **Use perspective to manipulate your field.**

Perspective can isolate the child against different fields. For instance, by shooting up at a child you can photograph him against a blue sky, setting off an idyllic moment of play. By shooting straight on you can eliminate a cluttered background, which might show from another perspective. By shooting down at the child you can include objects in the foreground that wouldn't otherwise show.

5. **Use perspective to manipulate available light.**

For instance, if you're shooting on a bright day with the sun high in the sky, you can eliminate long shadows on the face by positioning yourself above the subject and having him tilt his face up at you. Study how different perspectives cause the light to play off the child in various ways.

USING COLOR IN YOUR COMPOSITIONS

Color, or in the case of black-and-white photography, tonal value, is the final element of composition that you can use to manipulate the eyes of the viewer.

1. **Use contrasting colors between the subject and the field to lift the child off the background.** A child in a red coat against a stand of evergreens almost seems to pop out of the picture. But a child photographed in a green coat against green trees might fade into the background.

2. **Repeat spots of color for a unifying effect.** Using the same color family or tone in the main compositional elements creates a bold visual impact. For instance, a branch with pink flowers in the foreground, framing a child in a pink hat, can lead the eyes of the viewer to the child's face—the picture's center of interest.

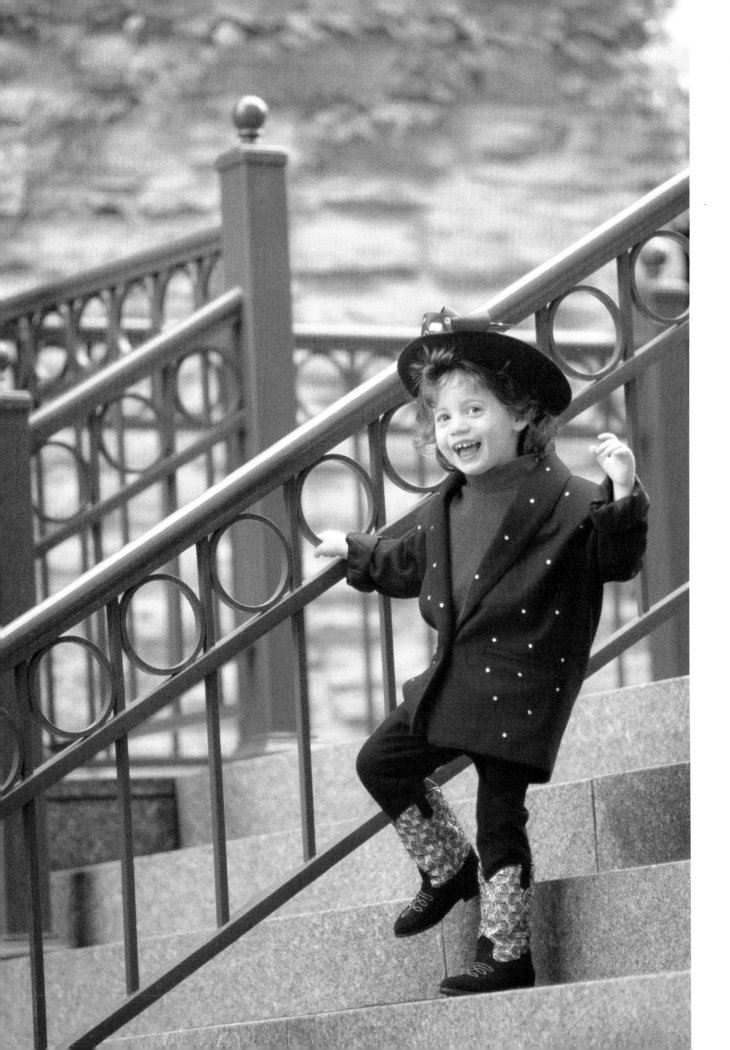

(Left.) This shot includes warm compositional elements that draw the eye in toward the subject. The orange leaves in the upper segment of the shot lead to the girl's red-trimmed hat, her pink shirt, and finally to her face. Had the leaves been a cool or neutral color, the composition would have had quite a different effect.

Overcast day; outdoors; Nikon 8008; Nikkor 180/2.8 AF lens; Fuji-chrome 400 (professional film).

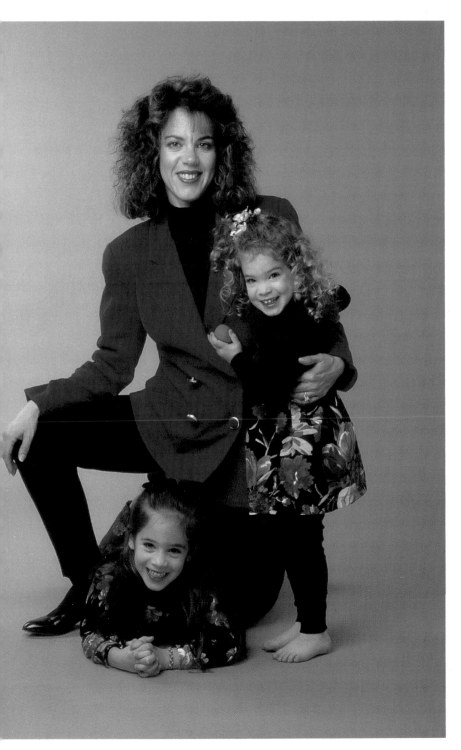

Multiple subjects should touch to create only one area of interest.

Strobes; studio; Nikon 8008; Nikkor 35-105mm zoom AF lens; Fuji Velvia 50.

This little girl's doll collection creates a foreground that frames her and draws the eyes in toward her face.

Available light; indoors; Nikon 8008; Nikkor 180/2.8 AF lens; Fuji Velvia 50.

Informal balance can liven up overall composition when several different shots are juxtaposed. The non-traditional cropping of this collage creates a feeling of energy and motion. If every shot were vertical and centered, the visual impact would have been considerably lessened.

Strobes; studio; Nikon 8008; Nikkor 35-105mm zoom AF lens; Kodak VPS III (professional film).

(Right.) Shooting down at a child can emphasize a mood of innocence or isolation and the child's small size.

Natural light; studio, Hasselbad 2.4 camera; 80mm lens; Kodak 200 print film.

(Left.) Shooting from the same height, or perspective, as these kids, puts us on their level, and helps us identify with them.

Strobes; studio; Nikon 8008; Nikkor 35-105mm zoom AF lens; Fuji Velvia 50.

This girl was shot for an annual report for Big Brothers and Big Sisters of America. We shot up at her to emphasize the fact that she is an athlete and academic achiever.

Strobes; studio; Nikon 8008; Nikkor 180/2.8 AF lens; Kodak Plus-X (professional film); printed on Agfa Portriga 118 matte paper and hand-colored with Marshall photo oils and pencils.

My favorite setup for shooting at home: The subject faces the window with white fill cards on either side of her, and a sheet of pink paper creates an innocuous background.

Available light; indoors; Nikon 8008; Nikkor 180/2.8 AF lens; Kodak Ektachrome 100 (professional film).

An age-old battle is being waged among photographers who champion one type of portraiture lighting over another. Any light is appropriate for children's portraits: hard or soft, natural or studio, and each has its joys and tribulations. The type of light you choose for a given portrait will in great part depend on the feeling you want to evoke. Light, perhaps more than any other single element of a picture, dictates its mood.

To use light effectively, learn to really *see* it. Start paying attention to the way sunlight looks at different times of the day and at different times of the year. How does light look reflected off the water or filtered through tree branches? How does the light from a north-facing window compare to the light from a south-facing window? Understanding the difference between hard and soft light will help you plan your portrait lighting, whether you're shooting outdoors, indoors, or in the studio: *hard light* comes from a small, direct light source; *soft light* comes from a large, diffused or indirect light source.

Pros

SHOOTING IN NATURAL LIGHT

• Natural outdoor light, used by a skilled photographer, can make unbelievably beautiful pictures. While natural light can be imitated in the studio, its subtlety is rarely equalled.

• What you see is approximately what you get; there's no need to guess or shoot Polaroids to predict your results.

• It's free, and you don't need to haul any heavy equipment.

Cons

• You have to take what you get — natural light dictates where and when you shoot.

• It can change in a split second; even a small, puffy cloud passing over the sun could change your exposure by one, two or more stops.

• You run the risk of having to reschedule because of bad weather. The parent of your subject should understand that a shoot in natural light is "weather permitting."

• You are always limited to certain times of day and certain ways to orient your subject. The options for when to shoot become more limited during fall and winter as the days grow shorter.

For best results

• While logic calls for posing your subject looking into the sun, this makes for a squinty-eyed, uncomfortable kid: orient your subject with his back to the sun and use a strobe to light his face; or orient the sun to one side of the child; shoot in open shade.

• Shoot at times of the day—and the year—when the sun is low in the sky to avoid dark eye sockets and long shadows under noses. Early morning, late afternoon and early evening during spring and fall are great times because of the sunlight's warm tone and gentle angle. Avoid shooting in the bright, harsh light of midday, especially solar noon.

• Take advantage of overcast days. Though many amateurs mistakenly avoid shooting when there's heavy cloud cover, this can be some of your most flattering light for human subjects because of its soft, even quality.

To manipulate natural light

• Use diffusion screens to soften direct sunlight.

• Use fill-flash to soften shadows and brighten up skin tones (see page 41 for a complete discussion).

• Use over-the-lens diffusers to soften overall contrast and skin texture.

• Use reflector cards to bounce light onto the subject, balancing the lighting and softening shadows.

**SHOOTING
WITH
AVAILABLE
LIGHT**

Available light can come from a window, skylight, lamp, fire, candle . . . anything. It can be natural sunlight or artificial lamplight.

Pros

• As with natural light, it doesn't cost you anything to use, and there's no heavy equipment.

• Its look is completely uncontrived; there's no worry about making it appear natural, as there often is with the use of studio light or camera-mounted flash units.

Cons

• Often, available light results from different combined sources that have very different color balance.

• There frequently isn't enough available light to make good, fine-grained pictures.

Here are two examples of natural sunlight. The picture above was made in the afternoon in autumn when the sun is relatively low in the sky. The picture at right was made in the summer in early evening — notice the warm, almost glowing quality of the light.

(Above.) Sunlight; outdoors; Nikon 8008; Nikkor 35-105mm zoom AF lens; Fuji Velvia 50.

(Right.) Sunlight; outdoors; Nikon 8008; Nikkor 180/2.8 AF lens; Kodak Ektachrome 100 (professional film).

For best results

- Be aware of the color balance of common available light sources and use corrective gels accordingly.

- When available light is low, use a fast, grainy film such as Kodak 1600 Ektapress film to capture the shot, rather than resorting to direct flash, as many of us are wont to do. What you lose in fine-grained detail you'll gain in mood and beauty. If the light is very low, consider shooting a chrome film such as Fujichrome 400 professional film and push processing to gain 3 or more stops. (See page 94 for push processing information.)

- When you must augment available light, it's important to make the extra light seem natural and logical, in other words, as if it naturally existed as part of the setting. The additional light shouldn't overpower the available light, but should be the same or slightly weaker f-stop. Augmented light can mimic some other common light source, such as a window or a skylight.

To manipulate available light

- Use a camera-mounted flash unit for fill-flash and/or bouncing off a reflector, wall or the ceiling.

- Use portable tungsten lights, called floods or hot lights, to fill in shadows or brighten skin tones.

(Far left.) Available light; warehouse; Nikon 8008; Nikkor 108/2.8 AF lens; Fuji Velvia 50.

(Left.) Available light; studio; Nikon 8008; Nikkor 180/2.8 AF lens; 3M Scotch 1000 (chrome film), push processed 1 stop.

• Use lens-mounted color corrective gels to neutralize yellow tint in tungsten-lit shots and green tint in fluorescent-lit shots.

Electronic flash makes shots possible when the light level is too low to make them any other way. It can be used to raise the overall light level or to fill in shadows on the subject's face without overpowering existing light.

SHOOTING WITH CAMERA-MOUNTED OR HAND-HELD FLASH

Pros

• There's always enough light (provided your subject is within the recommended range) so you never have to miss a shot.

• You can use it to freeze action.

• It's lightweight, battery operated and easy to use anywhere, especially in comparison to studio strobe units. Rechargeable batteries can be used with some units.

• It's color balanced to approximate daylight for use with daylight film.

• It creates a softer, more natural effect if it's bounced off another surface such as a wall or the ceiling rather than being aimed directly at the subject.

Cons

• Direct flash can be very hard and unnatural looking, creating undesirable shadows, washing out skin tones, flattening the overall appearance of a picture, and destroying detail in areas of highlights.

• Most amateur and some professional cameras have their flash mounts too close to the lens, which causes the light to enter the subject's eyes and bounce directly back at the lens, creating what is commonly known as red eye.

• It cannot match the softness or subtlety of natural light.

• Unlike natural light where what you see is what you get, it's hard to visualize what effect you're achieving with flash.

For best results

• Soften flash light by pointing the unit straight up and away from the child and bouncing it off a reflector card, the ceiling or even your hand.

• Rather than using the flash at full power, which raises the overall light level and overpowers existing light, use a technique called *fill-flash* where the flash is set at approximately the same f-stop as the existing light. This will brighten skin tones and fill in shadows. Fill-flash is achieved in different ways with different cameras and flash units, so consult your manufacturer's instruction manual to learn how your equipment performs this useful effect.

- With the aid of a flash extension cord of at least three feet, detach the flash unit from the camera mount and hold it at a 45 to 90 degree angle from the subject to mimic window light. You may hand hold the flash unit yourself, enlist the help of an assistant, or mount it on a stand.

To manipulate a camera-mounted flash

- Bounce the flash off of your hand, a reflector card, the ceiling or a wall.
- Use the flash unit away from the camera, either hand held or attached to a stand.
- Use flash or lens-mounted color corrective filters to warm and mimic available light color balance. I recommend 8 1EF, but there are many filters available. Experiment to find the ones you prefer.

SHOOTING WITH STROBE LIGHT Professional photographers use strobe lights in the studio and on location. Strobes are much like larger, more powerful cousins to the camera-mounted electronic flash. Studio strobes require power boxes that plug into ordinary 110-watt wall outlets. These boxes commonly provide from 800 to 2400 watt seconds of power, which can be divided among one to three or more light heads.

Pros

- There's always enough light.

Two examples of camera-mounted electronic flash: fill-flash bounced off a wall directional; fill-flash camera-mounted and pointed directly at the side-lit subject directional. Notice how much softer the effect is than that of camera-mounted flash lighting as it is commonly used.

(Left.) Available light augmented with fill-flash; indoors; Nikon FE2; Nikkor 180/2.8 AF lens; Fuji Velvia 50; #3 tiffen soft filter.

(Right.) Available light augmented with fill-flash; indoors; Nikon FE2; Nikkor 180/2.8 AF lens; Fujichrome 100 (professional film).

- As with electronic camera-mounted flash, it freezes action.
- With different types of light heads, color corrective filters and reflectors, limitless lighting effects are possible.

Cons

- As with electronic camera-mounted flash, it's hard to visualize what your finished result will be. Professional photographers often rely on Polaroid tests to see what they're getting, but Polaroid equipment and film is expensive.
- The power packs and the need for electrical outlets make them awkward to take along on location.

To manipulate strobe light

- Use the strobe mounted with light modifiers including white umbrellas, soft boxes, grid spots, barn doors and more.
- Use foamcore board to reflect light and black fabric or cardboard (also called gobos) to block or absorb it.
- See chapter 8 for more on strobes, light modifiers, reflectors and gobos.

When photographing a child, regardless of whether you're using natural, available or studio light, your challenge usually is to capture a moving subject.

In the home, a lighting setup I like is to place the subject by a window and bounce the natural light around with reflectors. The backdrop and reflectors create a comfortable little space that keeps the child more or less in position.

After much experimentation in the studio I've developed a setup that allows for some depth in the lighting, lets the child move around, and limits his movement at the same time. With this setup, the reflector and the gobo form physical boundaries that help keep the kids centered on the backdrop. I know of one photographer whose assistants handhold the light heads and reflectors, and when the kid moves, so do they. Unfortunately, hiring enough assistants to do this is a luxury few of us can afford.

On location, however, it's easy to have one person slightly off camera hold a white

These portraits illustrate the different looks you can
create in the studio with strobes. In the first shot (left)
the strobes allowed me to freeze fast action; in the second (above), I used them to imitate window light; and
in the third (right) to create a hard dramatic look.

(Left.) Strobes; studio; Nikon 8008, Nikkor 35-105mm zoom AF
lens; Kodak Plus-X (professional film); printed on Agfa Portriga
118 matte paper and hand-colored with Marshall photo oils and
pencils.

(Above and right.) Strobes; studio; Nikon 8008; Nikkor 35-105mm
zoom AF lens; Fuji Velvia 50.

or matte gold reflector and follow the child's movements. Fill-flash is also a great way to light a moving subject on location, since it evens out but doesn't overwhelm the natural light and maintains the density of the background.

You can also use 4×8 diffusion screens on location (see also chapter 8). Use them outdoors both over and beside the child to soften direct sunlight. Indoors, use them as a covering on the inside or outside of a window to lessen the contrast between incoming natural light and the light in the rest of a room.

• **Don't overlight the child.** Some photographers, especially beginners, seem to fear shadows, and so they overlight. Instead, let both light and dark areas enhance the contour of a child's face. As a photographer of children, you have the amazing luxury of shooting people who have no wrinkles, few blemishes, no sagging jowls and no sunken or baggy eyes, so you can well afford lighting that's more dramatic and more interesting.

• **Don't use too many light sources.** More isn't better when it comes to lighting. The best setups involve the use of only one or two light sources. The most you could possibly ever need for a full-length studio shot is three. If you use too many light sources, you could wind up with a flat picture, or one with too many undesirable shadows.

• **Use reflectors instead of lights for fill whenever possible.** It's amazing how much light a simple white card can bounce: I never realized how valuable they were until I shot a wedding for a friend on a bright but overcast day. I used available light. All the candids of the guests at the outdoor luncheon looked great, but the posed shots of the wedding party showed bags under eyes and generally tired skin tones. Upon closer observation, I realized that the white tablecloths had acted as fill cards, reflecting the available light up onto the guests' faces, and saving the shots.

• **Don't rely on direct flash for everything.** With a little thought and planning, you can manipulate available light or bounce your flash to create flattering and dramatic lighting.

There is no one correct exposure at which to shoot a given picture. In fact, by changing exposure you can achieve an enormous range of moods with the very same light.

For the greatest control over exposure use a hand-held light meter instead of your automatic through-the-lens metering, which can be fooled. The following are general rules for setting exposure in different lighting situations—as usual, meant to be bent or broken as you see fit.

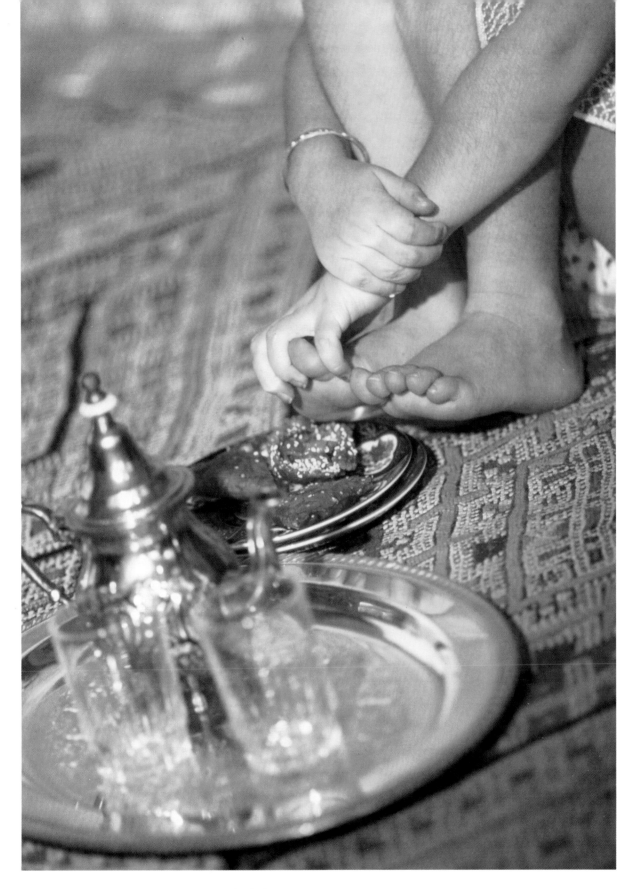

Tungsten light is warmer than strobe light, which is balanced to daylight. In this shot, tungstens were used to mimic the warm light of the late afternoon sun.

Tungsten theatrical lights; studio; Nikon 8008; Nikkor 180/2.8 AF lens; Fuji Velvia 50.

My favorite studio light setup allows the child maximum freedom of movement. My gobo and reflector do double duty, controlling light, but also confining the subject to the backdrop, which acts as a security "nook."

Strobes; studio; Nikon 8008; Nikkor 35-105mm zoom AF lens; Kodak Plus-X 100 (professional film); printed on Agfa Portriga 118 matte paper and hand-colored with Marshall photo oils and pencils, artist's oils.

When your subject is isolated against a *dark background*, your through-the-lens averaging meter reads this background and thinks the picture requires more light than it really does, resulting in an overexposed shot. To avoid this, use one of these techniques: If your camera has an exposure compensation feature, stay in the automatic mode and simply set the compensation at minus ½ to 1 stop. If you haven't got this feature, you'll need to go to a manual mode, and using your through-the-lens averaging meter, get a reading off a medium-toned object in the shot or your 18 percent gray card placed next to the child, and set your aperture accordingly. If your camera offers both center-weighted and matrix metering, set it on center-weighted to get a reading more true to your subject.

The opposite metering techniques are used when your subject is against a *white or very bright background*. To avoid underexposing with a through-the-lens meter, set your compensation for plus ½ to 1 stop; choose matrix over center-weighted metering when possible; and as always, use a hand-held meter and manual mode for best results.

If your subject has a very *dark complexion* or is wearing *dark clothing*, especially against a bright or light field, compensate plus ½ to 1 stop; use center-weighted metering or a hand-held meter and manual mode.

If your subject has a very *light complexion*, and/or is wearing *light clothing*, compensate minus ½ to 1 stop, use center-weighted metering, or hand-held meter and manual mode.

For *sidelit* subjects compensate plus ½ to 1 stop from the average through-the-lens meter reading to capture detail in the shadowed areas.

When your subject is *evenly lit from the front*, and the tone of the background doesn't deviate grossly from the tone of your subject, shoot on your average meter reading from either your through-the-lens or hand-held meter.

When your subject is *backlit*, compensate plus 1 and even 2 stops from the average reading from any type of meter.

When you shoot with a *zoom lens*, the amount of light allowed to enter the lens decreases as the focal length increases. You will need to set your compensation feature to allow for ½ stop more light, or set your aperture accordingly in a manual mode, when shooting at your longest focal length.

THE RISKS OF BRACKETING

Bracketing is the practice of shooting the same shot at many different exposures to insure you capture at least one shot at the optimum exposure. When shooting any other subject except children, my motto is, "Bracket like crazy!" But a child's ephem-

(Left.) It's easy to make skin tones sparkle and soften shadows when shooting on location by enlisting a helper to hold a white reflector card just outside the frame, aimed upward at the subject's face.

Sunlight; outdoors; Nikon 8008; 180/2.8 AF lens; Fujichrome 200 (professional film).

(Right.) Don't put away your camera just because it's not picnic weather! This great shot was made on an overcast day with soft, diffused light.

Sunlight; outdoors; Nikon 8008; Nikkor 180/2.8 AF lens; Fuji Reala 160 (professional film).

eral moods, gestures and expressions make bracketing a dangerous proposition. What if you lose that one-in-a-million expression because it happened in the frame that is 2 stops underexposed? Even with automatic bracketing, your results can be iffy.

Don't panic! There are ways to insure your exposures work:

• Use print films that have wide exposure latitudes, such as Fuji Reala and Kodak Vericolor III, so you get good results even if your metering is a little off.

• Shoot chrome film and ask your photo lab to process only the first foot or so of film so you can examine the results (this is called a *clip test*), and adjust the processing on your balance if necessary. (Read more about clip tests in chapter 10.)

• Use bounced flash, which gives you control over the exposure, looks relatively natural, always gives the subject a predictable amount of light, and won't change the density of your background. Avoid using direct flash, which washes out skin tones and can make the background go dark.

HOW TO IMPROVE YOUR LIGHTING SKILLS

To improve your lighting skills, find interesting lighting situations in photographs in magazines and printed material. Study and re-create them. The photo itself often tells exactly how it was lit.

• Look at the catch lights (the light reflections in the iris) in a subject's eyes. By noting their number, position, size and shape, you can tell how many light sources were used, where they were positioned in relation to the subject, and how and if they were bounced. Umbrellas cause a round catch light, within which you can frequently see the spines. Soft boxes make a square or rectangular catch light. Windows often make a vaguely rectangular, irregular catch light. Direct light makes a round, tiny catch light. Sometimes white foamcore reflectors can be seen in the eyes, as well.

• The quality of the contour on a face tells you a lot about the light sources, as well. Flat light with

hard shadows under the nose and jaw usually results from a small, direct light source such as a bare strobe head. Softer, more pronounced contouring results from larger, bounced sources such as umbrellas and soft boxes. (*Note:* The size of the light source is relative to its distance from the subject. A large light source placed far away from the subject will behave as a small light source.)

• The angles at which shadows fall on the face give away the position of the light sources. Overhead light causes shadows beneath the nose and jaw—the longer the shadows, the higher the position of the light. Lights positioned far to one side will cast shadows on the opposite side of the face—the farther to the side, the darker the shadow.

Some lighting setups you can re-create are included in chapter 11.

If you ask kids where they would like to be photographed, they'll give you plenty of great ideas. My niece and nephew suggested this abandoned, burned-out foundation of a '20s speakeasy for a location.

Sunlight; outdoors; Nikon 8008; Nikkor 180/2.8 zoom AF lens; Fuji Reala 100 (professional film).

When shooting on location (not in a studio), choose a place that tells something about **ON LOCATION** the child's interests: the zoo, a fire station, a farm, a campsite. If you run out of ideas, ask your young subject for some — he's bound to have more than a few!

Scout out the location, looking for backgrounds that are photogenic, add interest to the shot, flatter but don't compete with your subject, and work for your lighting plans. Foliage, buildings, fences, fountains and sporting events can all provide good backgrounds. Or just let the child go where he likes and follow him around. He'll find places that he'll be comfortable in, and you'll capture some great expressions as he explores his new environment.

One way to guarantee that the background won't overpower your subject or look cluttered is to use a lens with a long focal length (105 to 180mm), or use your regular lens at its most open aperture. The objects in the background (and the foreground) will be rendered in soft focus, so even if the location is cluttered or complex, the subject will be separated from the field.

When you're shooting at home, use backgrounds that are near windows so you can shoot with natural light. Isolate the child against a bare wall, in front of a window, in his bed, and amid his toys or collections. If he's playing on the floor, stand up on a piece of furniture and shoot down on him to eliminate background clutter. Follow your child out into the yard to take advantage of sunlight or open shade, the swing set, the garden and all of nature's wonders.

Watch for electrical outlets, switch plates, garden hoses and other common household objects that would be distracting if included in the picture. It's easy to forget about these little things because we see them every day and so become blind to them. But if they crop up in a shot right over little Johnny's head, you'll wish you'd paid attention.

When you photograph a child in his home, you have the advantage of the comfort he feels being on his own turf, and you'll be able to capture natural expressions most easily. It can also contribute to the sentimental value of a picture when the child is portrayed in his own environment. You also have the option of using a mini backdrop to create a professional studio look in the child's home.

Foliage and architectural elements provide good backgrounds. Notice how, in this picture with a train background, the focal length of the lens visually lifts the subject off the field.

Overcast day; outdoors; Nikon 8008; Nikkor 180/2.8 AF lens; Kodak Ektachrome 1600 (amateur film).

The child's own home can provide many suitable backgrounds. This shot made with a wide lens places the subject almost comically in the foreground, while capturing his bedroom in the background.

Available light augmented with fill-flash; indoors; Nikon 8008; Nikkor PC 35mm lens; Fujichrome 100 (professional film).

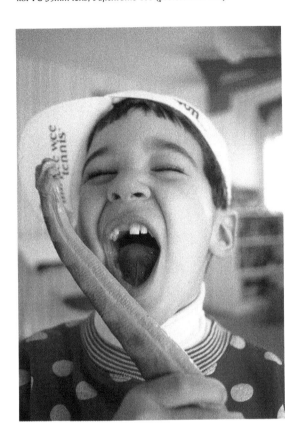

BACKDROPS FOR THE HOME AND STUDIO For shooting in homes and on location, backdrops should be no larger than 6 × 8 feet primarily because transporting larger ones is awkward. A plain or patterned sheet, a few yards of fabric, or a large, colored piece of poster board can all be attractive backgrounds for head shots. These mini drops can be taped to the wall with artist's or photographer's tape (available at art supply stores), or they can be hung from homemade or commercially available portable backdrop holders. (See page 58 for information on backdrop holders.) For easy storage and transportation of mini drops, tape one end around an appropriately sized wooden dowel. These can be hung unrolled in a closet between uses or rolled up around the dowel to transport without wrinkling.

An enormous range of backdrops is available for studio use, providing different colors, textures and tones to complement your subjects. Some are disposable; others are durable. They range from the simplicity of white seamless paper to impressionistic, mottled canvas to literal depictions of granite façades, street scenes or meadows.

Remember when you're shopping for backdrops:

• Colors and texture should enhance the subject (especially skin tones), and not distract from the clothing.

• Size should be appropriate to your shooting needs. Full-body action portraits

Follow the child around as he explores his environment. You'll be rewarded with shots like this one taken at a maritime museum in Maine.

Available light; partially enclosed; Nikon 8008; Nikkor 35-105mm zoom AF lens; Kodak VPS III 160 (professional film).

The urban-looking, weathered wall adds interest without distracting from the subject.

Overcast day; outdoors; Nikon 8008; Nikkor 180/2.8 AF lens; Kodak Ektachrome 1600 (amateur film).

should be shot on a drop no smaller than 9×22 feet. Head shots should be photographed against a drop at least 4×5 feet for individuals or 5×8 feet for multiple subjects. The effect created by the drop should not appear contrived or clichéd; for instance, I personally think that literal depictions of skies, environmentals and scenics should be left for location work.

When selecting backdrops for the studio, be aware of what the look of your drop says to people—what seems fresh or friendly to you might strike others as overly commercial, "photo mill," old-fashioned, etc. Study different backdrop styles through the years. See what other local studios are offering in the way of backdrops. And beware of trends—don't play follow the leader.

WHERE TO BUY OR RENT BACKDROPS Ordinary seamless paper is the least expensive backdrop, comes in many colors including white, pastels and brights, and can be purchased from your professional photographic supplier. Stock drops, such as mottled canvas, are available from photographic supply houses and mail-order manufacturers that cater to portrait photographers. Check display and classified ads in photographic trade periodicals. If you live in a metropolitan area, you may find local artists and set designers who sell ready-made canvas drops.

Order custom-made backdrops from mail-order manufacturers, although ideally

Smaller versions of most of the studio backdrops described on page 58 ("Recommended Backdrops") can be used in the home. Here, a piece of black velvet is an easy-to-use, flattering background.

Strobe; indoors; Nikon 8008; Nikkor 180/2.8 lens; Fuji Velvia 50; #1 tiffen soft filter.

you should find a local artist who specializes in backdrops and with whom you can work closely.

If you need a special backdrop that you'll only use once or twice, renting it may be the answer. Backdrop manufacturers usually stock popular styles for rental, and you can even order a custom-made backdrop to rent (usually at half the purchase price).

The same supply houses that sell backdrops through classified ads in photography magazines also frequently offer their products for rent. Frequently their rental price includes shipping and three days' usage. Locally, check with professional photographic retailers and rental houses. Even if they don't carry rental drops, they should be able to refer you to someone who does.

Some photographers elect to paint their own backdrops to save money and have total artistic control. For inspiration, browse mail-order backdrop catalogs. For specific instruction on painting techniques, your library should have books on theatrical scenic painting, theatrical set building and faux finishes.

As in all things, start out with the best materials: seamless cotton muslin, duck cloth or canvas (the most durable), latex paints, natural sea sponges, cotton rags and good-quality brushes.

**PAINT YOUR
OWN DROP**

ALTERNATIVE DROPS

You don't necessarily need giant canvas drops or seamless paper for every picture. Head shots can be featured against solid or patterned fabric or rugs; plain, unpainted sheets or muslin (use your imagination to drape the fabric for added texture); black velvet; layers of torn or wrinkled paper—almost anything else you can think of.

BACKDROP HOLDERS

Most of the photographers I know (including myself) have makeshift backdrop stands, slapped together from broom handles, old light stands, rope and pulleys—you name it.

Portable, easy-to-use background holders are available, manual or motorized, which can hold one to four drops. If you never leave your home or studio, you can probably get by with a homemade model. But if you shoot in other people's homes, as many child portrait photographers do, you'll want professional equipment. Ask at your professional photographic supplier for catalogs and information, or check publications for classifieds from mail-order houses.

RECOMMENDED BACKDROPS

I use the following backdrops and find them indispensable in my commercial and portrait work with kids:

• White seamless paper, 9 feet wide. Fully lit, it's naturally white. Lit approximately 1 stop less than the subject, it is pale gray. Lit with lights covered with colored gels, it can be any number of colors.

• Medium dark, warm-toned brown, mottled canvas backdrop, 12 × 24 feet. With different lighting it appears light to dark, heavily or softly mottled. It is flattering to skin tones and most clothing colors.

• Black velvet, 4 × 8 feet. A beautiful, dramatic backdrop for head shots.

• Assorted pastel and bright color seamless papers, 9 feet wide. Inexpensive and easy to store, these papers are used for portraiture and commercial shooting.

• Wrinkled, unpainted cotton muslin, 10 × 20 feet. Ideal for draping for different effects.

• Assorted fabric, approximately 4 × 9 feet. Provides a range of looks and colors from old-fashioned or retro to contemporary.

• Whether you're selecting drops for full-length or head shots, for the studio or home, remember that your background should first and foremost complement your subject.

These four photos show the backdrops I use most often in my studio: white seamless paper, a mottled brown canvas, colored seamless paper, and wrinkled muslin.

Strobe; studio; Nikon 8008; 35-105mm zoom AF lens; Fuji Velvia 50.

This whimsically styled shot was created as a portrait for the family's home and was also later used on a holiday card with the legend, "Have a Magical, Mystical Christmas."

Strobes; studio; Nikon FE2; Nikkor 35-105mm zoom AF lens; Kodak Plus-X (professional film); printed on Agfa Portriga 118 matte paper and hand-colored with Marshall photo oils, pencils, and artist's oils.

In photographic jargon, to *style* a picture means to create, procure and arrange clothing and objects to appear in the picture. As a portrait photographer, you may select backdrops, furniture, props and clothing to enhance your portrayal of your subject. As a parent/amateur photographer, though you might not have thought of it in these terms before, you style your candids. Even the simplest shots — say, of a naked baby — are styled.

A commercial photographer styles a shot for maximum visual impact and surprise. More often than not, the objective of a commercial photo is to sell a product. When a child is featured in this type of work, the shot is styled so the child flatters the product.

Conversely, with portraiture, objects are chosen to flatter the child. A favorite toy (no matter how ragged) might soothe her, lend sentimental value to the portrait, and provide simple visual interest or a more pleasing composition.

A portrait photographer might also benefit from styling designed to achieve the element of surprise or whimsy. Handing a child a new object a second or two before you shoot can capture genuine moments of surprise. Items as simple as pennies, sea shells, balls, flowers, blades of grass, or bells evoke expressions of sheer wonder and delight. Tiny objects such as a penny barely read at all in the finished photo and are used solely to evoke an expression. Larger objects can be used to add color, texture and strong graphic elements.

CHILD AS STYLIST

I always encourage parents to bring at least three different outfits to the studio and to let the child select what they want to wear. Some of the photos with the best artistic impact have been styled by the children themselves. Who else but a child would put together a flower girl dress, high-top sneakers, heart-shaped sunglasses, and a soccer ball? In addition to creating great visual interest, allowing the child to style her own shoot also makes for a better portrait as it literally portrays the child's personality and interests.

One mom who scheduled a photo session at my studio called me thinking she had a problem. It seemed her eight-year-old son wanted to bring his tux and his

(Right.) This boy came to his photo session in Western duds. The scenery was added with artist's oils after the shot was made.

Strobes; studio; Nikon 8008; Nikkor 35-105mm AF zoom lens; Kodak Plus-X 100 (professional film); printed on Afga Portriga 118 #2 contrast paper; hand-colored with artist's oils, oil pastels, and oil-based pencils.

(Left.) Even a simple shot such as this was styled so it would be compositionally pleasing.

Strobes; studio; Nikon 8008; Nikkor 180/2.8 AF lens; Fuji Velvia 50.

new dress suit to the shoot, while her twelve-year-old refused to wear anything but sweatshirts and jeans. She wanted to know if she should force a compromise and make them each wear complementary clothing in the shots of the two of them together because she was afraid they wouldn't "match." I encouraged her to let them wear whatever they chose, to let their personalities come out instead of being concerned about matching outfits. The resulting photos are some of my favorite to date.

If you decide to allow the child to be your stylist, give her carte blanche to choose anything she likes. The results won't be pleasing to either of you if you say, "Okay on the cowboy outfit, but eighty-six those funny looking chaps." We've had success with fairies, cowboys, pumpkins, bunnies, spiders and more. Trust the child's sensibilities completely.

You may be afraid costumes will detract from the goal of a portrait. But dress up is a big part of a child's life, and just as adults sometimes seem to find it easier to "be themselves" when disguised at a costume party, so is a child very much himself in a costume.

PLAN AHEAD   The old Boy Scout motto, "Be prepared," really applies to photographic styling. There's nothing worse than the sinking feeling you get when you realize, "Gee, if only

The little yellow toy did double duty in this portrait:
It was the youngest brother's security toy, so it lent
sentimental value, and it added just the spot of color
that was needed.

Strobes; studio; Nikon 8008; Nikkor 35-105mm zoom AF lens;
Fuji Velvia 50.

we'd had Susie's security duckie, this could've been a great shot," or, "We need just a spot of color here, too bad we don't have anything." For portrait sessions I always ask parents to bring any and all favorite objects, from toys and books to sporting goods and musical instruments. I've had people show up at the studio with suitcases full of stuff. Some of it we use, some we don't. But my clients agree with me when I say that it's better to have too many options than not enough. I always keep an assortment of photogenic balls, hats, flowers and toys at the studio in case we need them. And, I always try to use the child's own objects in portraits whenever possible, but sometimes a strange new toy charms the child into a more playful mood.

For commercial work and other more elaborate setups, I plan out the shot in my mind and then bring along anything I think might even remotely come in handy. At any given moment the hatch of my car might contain antique Coca-Cola crates, colored scarves, bales of hay, inner tubes, carved coconuts — anything.

BUT HANG LOOSE Now that I've told you to plan ahead, I'm going to contradict myself and tell you to "hang loose" as well. It's important not to be too rigid, nor to have your shoot too thoroughly planned, or you may become completely oblivious to serendipitous objects in your environment that may create that magic glue that makes all the elements of a really great photo come together. For instance, I was on location in downtown Minneapolis shooting a five-year-old "puppy yuppie" in a Brooks Brothers suit with loafers and no socks, a *Wall Street Journal* under his arm, and wire-rim glasses. I had planned to shoot him on a busy street with a yellow cab in the background. As it happened, this was easier said than done. Cabs in Minneapolis seem to come in blue, white, blue and white, gray — any color but yellow. When I finally found a yellow one

This girl did her own charming and surprising propping for this portrait, which hangs in the family's entryway at home.

Strobes; studio; Nikon FE2; Nikkor 35-105mm zoom AF lens; Kodak Plus-X (professional film); printed on Agfa Portriga 118 matte paper and hand-colored with Marshall photo oils and pencils, and artist's oils.

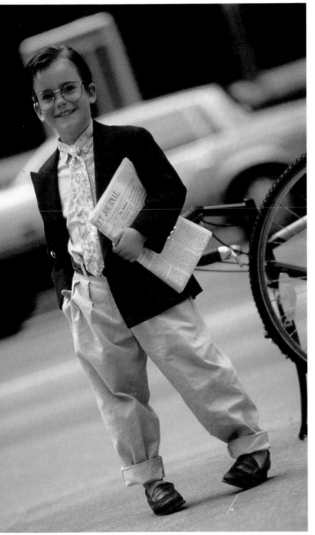

Plan ahead for your props and styling, but don't be so rigid that you fail to take advantage of dumb luck. In this shot, a bicycle that happened to be at our location added a great compositional element and enhanced the urban feeling.

Sunlight; outdoors; Nikon 8008; Nikkor 180/2.8 AF lens; Kodachrome 200 (professional film).

**Scattered flowers and a bright ribbon add color and
heighten the pensive quality of this shot.**

Strobes; studio; Nikon FE2; Nikkor 35-105mm zoom AF lens;
Kodak Plus-X (professional film); printed on Agfa Portriga 118
matte paper and hand-colored with Marshall photo oils and pencils, and artist's oils.

and positioned my subject in front of it, I became annoyed when I discovered a ten-
speed locked to a street sign in my frame and began thinking out ways to shoot around
it. Then as I was considering this, the subject's mom said, "That bike would look kind
of neat in the shot, wouldn't it?" Bingo.

You don't need to search for clever or ridiculous props to add the unexpected to your
photos. Sometimes objects that traditionally appear in photos of children can seem
new and exciting when handled differently. Consider how you can style these common
objects:

**ORDINARY
PROPS IN A
NEW LIGHT**

• Flowers are often seen in pictures of pretty little girls in frilly dresses. But what
if the girl were dressed in jeans, throwing the flowers up in the air, holding them
dropped casually at her side, as if she's forgotten them, or standing amidst them
scattered on the floor? Give the (nonpoisonous) flowers to a baby or toddler to hold
but stand close by to retrieve them in case your subject decides they look good enough
to eat. A small child will most assuredly do something unconventional with them, such
as playing "sword fight" or pulling them apart, and you'll have a whimsical photo.
Use unusually large flowers (sunflowers, giant tulips, and bird-of-paradise flowers are
good) to emphasize the smallness of a child. Use wildflowers or flowers from your
own garden, instead of the showy, more obvious store-bought hybrids for an unexpected look. Wrap the stems with ribbons, or tear off the stems and tuck the blossoms
into socks, pockets, hair, up sleeves and in collars. Let the child peek through the
flowers into the camera.

• Hats and toddlers might result in any number of things. A child might hold it,
wave it, stand on it, toss it up in the air, play peek-a-boo behind it, pull it down over
her ears, put it on upside down . . . the list goes on. The hat could be too big or too
small. It could be a fireman's hat, a baseball cap, or a paper crown of the child's own
making. The child could don lots of hats in a stack. Sometimes a hat simply held in
the hands can add a striking, graphic element.

• Musical instruments are endlessly intriguing to kids, as well as being objects of
beauty in their own right. The child doesn't have to be a virtuoso to be photographed
with a musical instrument. He doesn't even have to know how to hold it. Shots of the
child exploring a shiny trumpet or a violin and trying to play it can be charming, and
revealing of the child's personality.

• Ribbons can be fixed into a little girl's hair, of course. But she could also wave
them in the air like streamers, dance with them, tuck them into a pocket, hold a
bunch of them like a bouquet, or wind herself up in them.

• Sunglasses can be worn in the conventional way and peered over, tucked into the front of a shirt, or pushed back up onto the head. One girl at my studio managed to wear a record six pairs at once. Take care not to shoot too many pictures of the kids wearing glasses. They are a lot of fun as a prop, but they cover up one of the most interesting and expressive of facial features — the eyes.

• Sporting equipment of almost every type has been inside our studio, but it takes a little extra care to compose with. Skis are hard to fit into a pleasing composition; overeager skaters can fall down; balls and bats are hazardous near cameras and lighting equipment. But it's well worth the extra energy and caution to portray the child with the uniforms and equipment from her sport(s) of choice, because the zeal and sincerity she pours into its pursuit will be evident in the picture. If the child is active in

This little violinist was eager to include her instrument in her portrait.

Overcast day; outdoors; Nikon 8008; Nikkor 180/2.8 lens; Kodachrome 400 (professional film); push processed 3 stops.

Sporting equipment can give the child something to do in a portrait and tells you about his interests.

(Left.) Strobes; studio; Nikon 8008; Nikkor 35-105mm zoom AF lens; Kodak VPS III (professional film).

(Below.) Strobes; studio; Nikon 8008; Nikkor 35-105mm zoom AF lens; Fuji Velvia 50.

Ethnic identity portraits help us stay in touch with our roots, and emphasize our uniqueness. Anyone can have an ethnic identity portrait made; we all belong to ethnic groups.

(Left.) Strobes; studio; Nikon 8008; Nikkor 35-105mm zoom AF lens; Fuji Velvia 50.

(Right.) Tungsten theatrical lights; studio; Nikon 8008; Nikkor 180/2.8 AF lens; Fuji Velvia 50.

several sports, photograph her holding equipment and wearing parts of uniforms from all of them.

• Ethnic objects and clothing are integral to what I call "ethnic pride portraits," in which children born in the U.S., abroad, adopted or living with their biological families, don clothing and hold objects representing their ethnic heritage. I became interested in making ethnic pride portraits after reading about a new Afrocentric school in Minneapolis. When my clients booked their portrait sessions, I invited them to bring along any ethnic outfits the children might have. I found that both the parents and the kids loved the idea, and most of them owned such outfits. A child needn't be a member of an ethnic minority to make an ethnic pride portrait.

• Toys, particularly a child's favorites, both calm and entertain the child while providing an evocative portrait element. The older, dirtier and more ragged the toy, the better. I believe in years to come the presence of such an object in a portrait will give it inestimable value to the child and later generations. In portraits and commercial pictures, old worn toys can be infinitely more beautiful than new. New toys just don't have the character, texture and warmth of the old. Consider scouring antique shops for teddy bears oozing stuffing, yellowed toy drums, bashed-around metal trucks, old-fashioned baby buggies, bikes, and anything else that catches your eye.

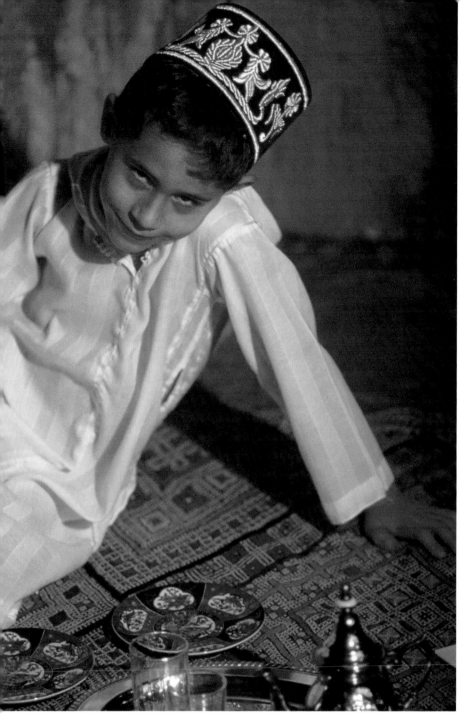

• Parents as props can make an individual portrait into a unique family portrait. A young dad once called me to make an appointment for a shoot three months in advance of his son's one year birthday so he could be sure to get the child's photo taken on the exact day. The family called me specifically because they wanted our specialty—full-body action shots. "I'm sure he'll be walking by then," the dad told me, as he hung up.

As fate would have it, the boy, a beautiful little redhead, wasn't even quite standing by himself, let alone walking. We tried standing him up on the seamless and stepping out of the shot at the last second, but he wilted to a sitting position every time. I suggested a family shot, so the parents could help him stand up by holding his hands, but they would have none of that. "What about photographing you two from the waist down?" I meant it as a joke, but then I thought, Why not? The resulting photo uses

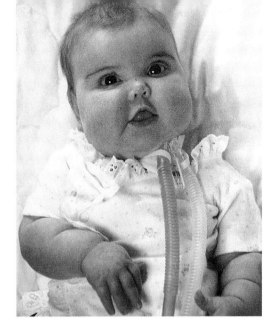

(Above.) Medical devices are appropriate in portraits of physically challenged kids whose quality of life is enhanced by them.

Available tungsten and fluorescent light; one tungsten "hot light" bounced off the ceiling; Nikon 8008; Nikkor 35-105mm zoom AF lens; Kodak 1600 Ektapress (professional film).

(Right.) Parents can be literal or figurative props in pictures of their offspring.

Strobes; studio; Nikon FE2; Nikkor 35-105mm zoom AF lens; Kodak Plus-X (professional film); printed on Agfa Portriga 118 matte paper and hand-colored with Marshall photo oils and pencils, and artist's oils.

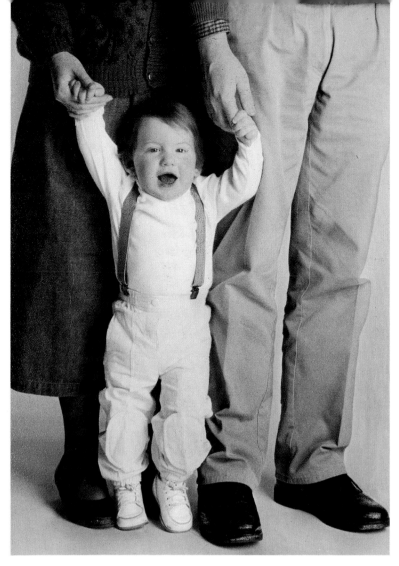

the parents, quite literally, as props. It shows how tiny the baby's hands are in comparison to those of his parents, and also shows an aspect of the relationship between family members.

• Makeup never makes a child look better because children are naturally beautiful. Makeup frequently gives photos a dated or "Hollywood" look. Costume and stage makeup, clown-white, and glitter, though, can be fun and playful.

• The right clothing can enhance a portrait. There's something inexplicably cute about a kid in a rain slicker and rubber boots. Likewise, a cloth coat, fake fur, a muff or mittens.

A portrait of a child in mom or dad's clothes is more than just cute—it also captures a universal experience of innocent play.

We've made many pictures of kids in their night clothes. It's a look parents love to capture on film. Sometimes we invite the kids to have pillow fights for the camera. . . you can probably imagine that we don't have to ask more than once.

Another favorite of parents is to make portraits of their kids in bathing suits, often replete with beach balls, sunglasses, and Mickey Mouse inner tubes. It's a fun way to capture those round little tummies, chunky knees and chubby toes.

• Messy hair, missing teeth, torn tights, holes in pants' knees, missing buttons, falling straps and untied shoelaces are some of my favorite props. I take advantage of

Swimming suits are a refreshing change from the dressy look of formal portraits and are fun for the kids to wear.

Strobes; studio; Nikon FE2; Nikkor 35-105mm zoom AF lens; Kodak Plus-X (professional film); printed on Agfa Portriga 118 matte paper and hand-colored with Marshall photo oils and pencils, and artist's oils.

These hand-colored shots use creative styling to highlight the child's natural grace and exuberance, and stretch the conventional concept of portraiture.

Strobes; Nikon FE2; Nikkor 35-105mm zoom AF lens; Kodak Plus-X (professional film); printed on Agfa Portriga 118 matte paper and hand-colored with Marshall photo oils and pencils, and artist's oils.

these things when they happen naturally, but I never contrive them. Most of my clients are in agreement with me on this, but some still want the kids to look picture perfect. One mom scheduled a photo session and then called back to cancel it because her little girl had lost a tooth. She wasn't going to have another professional portrait made of her until she had all her adult teeth. What a shame! Missing teeth are a natural part of childhood. If everyone shared that attitude, then 500 years from now, anthropologists looking at photographic records of our culture might think kids between six and twelve didn't exist.

• Birthmarks, freckles and other permanent features, which I consider a part of each child's beauty and individuality, should be included in portraits. On the other hand, while measles, chicken pox, bruises, bug bites, blemishes and the like are also natural parts of childhood, I have no qualms about retouching these out of a photo.

• Medical devices that are used by physically challenged kids are also appropriate props. I believe *portraits* should portray their subjects as individuals, and not try to make us all look the same or fit into the same mold. Therefore, when I shoot kids who are physically challenged, I don't try to make them look like able-bodied kids. They are beautiful as they are. And I don't try to hide or downplay any medical devices, such as respirators and wheelchairs, which help the kids get around and improve their quality of life. I believe it's important, when making portraits of all kids, to respect and to honestly represent all the qualities that make them unique.

Of course there will be times, like when you're shooting candids, when you won't have the opportunity to be picky about the objects or clothing of your subjects; sometimes when you see a great moment, you just have to shoot! But when you have the opportunity to plan, or the presence of mind to take advantage of a little serendipity in your environment, it can pay off in big dividends.

The equipment you choose greatly affects the type of photos you make. Here, a combination of strobe lights, autofocus camera, and a mid-length lens allowed me to freeze the action of this self-confident cowboy. A weaker light source, a manual-focus camera, or a lens with a long focal length might jeopardize a spontaneous shot.

Strobes; studio; Nikon 8008; Nikkor 35-105mm zoom AF lens; Kodak Plus-X 100 (b&w professional film).

I once met a photographer who had an unbelievably impressive array of photographic equipment—many different formats, lenses, enlargers—anything I could possibly imagine ever needing. *Wow*, I thought, *this guy must be a fantastic photographer*. I asked him to share some of his work with me. He admitted, rather sheepishly, that he hadn't made a picture in several years. "I guess I'm kind of a photo gearhead," he said. He admitted to reading photographic equipment catalogs the way kids read the Sears Wish Book at Christmastime.

Personally, I'm not a gearhead, but to me, a 180mm lens really is a thing of beauty. I appreciate equipment not for equipment's own sake, but for what I can say with it. Admiring equipment can be an expensive habit, but if you do your research and buy carefully, it can be worthwhile.

FEATURES TO GET IN A 35MM CAMERA

I find the 35mm camera perfect for the fast action of photographing children. It's lightweight and you don't need to stop and reload after only a few shots. Unless you plan on making a lot of shots for enlarging to larger than 11×14, you'll never need to aspire to a larger format. And with some of the new, fine-grained 35mm films, such as Kodak Ektar 25, you can now get results that rival those of larger format cameras even at enlargements of up to 16×20. I use the Nikon 8008 for almost all of my child photography. Although Nikon promotes it as their top-of-the-line amateur camera, it's popular among amateurs and pros alike. But Nikon isn't the only manufacturer that makes great 35mm cameras. You can make great pictures of kids with any brand of camera, as long as it's equipped with these features:

• **Autofocus** for the quickest possible response. Autofocus features are becoming more sophisticated all the time. Models are available that can track moving subjects and even anticipate the subject's movements.

• **Auto and manual exposure** so you can shoot without thinking about the exposure, or use artistic license in exposing your shots. Models are available with an automatic bracketing feature.

• **Motor drive** so that you don't have to pause to advance your film.

BEST LENSES
FOR
PHOTOGRAPHING
CHILDREN

BEST LENSES FOR PHOTOGRAPHING CHILDREN

For photographing children, there are two invaluable 35mm format lenses: a 35 to 105mm zoom, and a fixed 180mm. Both are available from all manufacturers. The zoom allows you maximum latitude in framing your shots, since from one position you can compose everything from full-length to head shots. It also lets you observe and shoot from a distance without being intrusive. I use the 35 to 105 zoom mainly in the studio to capture full- to three-quarter-length action shots.

The fixed 180mm makes it even easier to photograph kids unnoticed. Its most important feature is its ability to keep the subject in sharp focus with minimum distortion, while making the foreground and background soften into unfocused shapes and colors. While longer focal lengths, such as 200mm and even 300mm provide more softening of the field, they necessitate being very far away from your subject when you shoot, which limits their versatility. I almost always use the 180mm lens for shooting outside the studio, and for head shots in the studio.

As sort of a hobby, I like to read the ads in the newspaper classifieds for used photo equipment. It seems as though used 180mm lenses are almost never available. This leads me to believe that once a photographer uses one, he never wants to part with it.

When using the 180mm is impractical, but I still want a softer, more abstract background, I shoot with my zoom lens on its most open aperture (3.5) for its shallowest possible depth of field.

Don't try to save money by buying a cheap lens. If you do, you're guaranteed to regret it. Decide what type, fixed or zoom, and which focal length you want, and then buy the best one you can afford. I use a Nikkor 35 to 105mm AF, and a Nikkor 180mm AF.

MEDIUM AND LARGE FORMAT VIEW CAMERAS

Medium and large format cameras require more light and are heavier and more cumbersome to handle than 35mm cameras, making it more difficult to shoot active kids, especially in low light. No medium or large format cameras that I know of have autofocus features. And these cameras and their accessories tend to be very expensive. But there are some beautiful effects that can only be created with a 4 × 5 view camera, and if you're after fine grain, a medium format negative, at three to five times the size of a 35mm negative, provides quite superior results.

The medium format 6 × 4.5 camera, such as that made by Bronica or Mamiya, is a real boon for child photographers. Equipped and with automatic exposure, compact, relatively lightweight, and with the option of an eye-level viewfinder, this camera can go anywhere and do anything that the 35mm format can, and with a negative that's three-and-a-half times larger than with a 35mm.

Another useful medium format camera to consider is the 6×7, which, while not as handy as the 6×4.5 models, offers a negative three-and-one-half times the size of a 35mm negative as well, in the same proportion as an 8×10 print, so none of the image is wasted.

In general, the 6×4.5 cameras are good for jobs in which you want to hand hold your camera, and 6×7 cameras are good for use with a tripod.

Square negative medium format cameras such as the Hasselblad are my least favorite cameras for photographing children. Because my shots are typically vertical, I waste a large portion of the negative because of its square format, so I lose much of the finer grain it would otherwise provide over its smaller format cousins.

I use 150mm and 180mm lenses with medium format cameras for portraiture.

Large format (4×5, 8×10 and even larger) cameras are beautifully simple devices, because they are basically a movable box with a lens, shutter and a film plane. Unlike the 35mm cameras, which keep getting better and better with each new design, a large format camera need neither be new nor expensive to be good. You can pick up a virtually antique large format camera at a swap meet for a reasonable price, or buy a new bottom-of-the-line model at a low price, and still get good results.

I use a top-of-the-line Cambo 4×5 view camera, with a 210mm lens for shooting kids for commercial clients. I rarely use it for portraiture, except for Polaroid color transfers.

While the large format cameras are nice to have, they're certainly not a necessity for children's portraits. Though they provide the finest grain, they're really overkill for any enlargement up to 16×20.

ARTIFICIAL LIGHTS

Strobes, tungsten and camera-mounted flash are artificial lights used by portrait photographers. I, like most portrait photographers, rely heavily on strobe units because of their consistency and ability to stop action. So a good strobe unit should be dependable, require low maintenance, and have a short recycle time. (For instruction on how to use lights and their pros and cons for photographing children, see chapter 5.)

I use a Speedotron strobe. A local photographic equipment rental proprietor calls "Speedo" a great workhorse because it is durable and needs repair much less frequently than either of the other two popular—and more difficult to service— brands, Norman and Balcar. The Brown Line Speedo is a good unit for amateurs with up to 800 watt seconds (watt seconds are units used to measure power, or brightness of the light produced by strobes), and Black Line is good for pros, with special features

MUST-HAVE EQUIPMENT

To do anything well, you need quality tools. Anyone who wants to photograph children seriously should have the tools that will make it possible to translate their style and vision into pictures. Some of the equipment on this must-have list is expensive; some is only a few dollars. If cost is an issue, begin with the items you can afford now, and add items as you can. Must-haves for everyone include:
- 35mm camera with autofocus, automatic function and manual overrides
- midrange zoom lens, such as 35 to 105mm
- bounceable electronic flash with diffuser and extension cord
- reflectors (three 32×40-inch white foamcore sheets and two matte silver tagboard sheets)
- gobos (two 4×8-foot lengths of black fabric or two 32×40-inch black tagboard sheets)
- diffusion filter for lens (such as #1 Soft FX Tiffen)

- Kodak 8 1EF corrective color filter for lens
- site kit

In addition to the must-haves for everyone, studio photographers should have the following as well:
- strobe unit, at least 1200 watt seconds
- three light heads
- two 40-inch white umbrellas
- two 24×36-inch soft boxes
- three light stands
- hand-held light meter
- two diffusion screens
- extension for camera-mounted flash

Once you've acquired the must-haves, you can start compiling your wish list. Here are a few suggestions to get you started:
- 180mm lens
- Bronica 6×4.5 or other medium format camera

including adjustable power from as low as 50 watt seconds all the way up to 2400 watt seconds, and a fast recycle time. The broad power range allows you to fine-tune your lighting.

There are many different camera-mounted flash units to choose from. Many professional photographers use a Vivitar 285. Look for a unit that's compatible with your camera. An extension cord for using the flash away from the camera and a diffuser to soften the light are accessories that make good investments.

Tungsten floods and spotlights are rarely used by portrait photographers, so most photographic suppliers carry a limited selection. If you're interested in getting a more elaborate tungsten setup, see a theatrical supplier. Different wattages are available, and many models come complete with stands.

LIGHT MODIFIERS There are numerous ways to modify or control natural, available and strobe light, at home, on location, or in the studio to produce different qualities of light, from soft and diffused to extremely directional and hard. Experiment to find what you like the best. Light modifiers may be purchased new from mail-order and local retail photographic suppliers, or used from individuals or rental stores.

In general, umbrellas, soft boxes, and reflectors constructed of white materials are modifiers that provide the most flattering light for photographing children. Umbrellas and reflectors made of silver material provide more specular light, which can be uncomplimentary to skin texture and can create an unattractively cool color balance as well.

• **White umbrellas** are good, all-purpose reflectors for illuminating children and backdrops. For soft light, a large umbrella provides more diffusion. For harder light, a smaller umbrella is needed. To avoid spill (light coming off the umbrella in directions where you don't want it), buy white umbrellas with black backing material. Umbrellas are available in 30, 40, 45 and 54 inch sizes and are considerably lower priced than soft boxes.

• **Soft boxes** are my favorite light modifier for illuminating backdrops and children. Unlike umbrellas, which reflect light, soft boxes diffuse light to provide an effect that is soft but somewhat more directional. Some photographers object to the square catch lights caused by soft boxes, but there are new soft boxes on the market that create round and oval catch lights. Standard sizes (in inches) are 16×22, 24×32, 36×48 and 54×72.

• **Fill cards** can be made from white foamcore board, or white or matte gold tagboard. Tagboard comes in 3×4-foot sheets, and foamcore comes in up to 4×8-foot pieces. Both are available at most art supply stores.

• **Diffusion screens** are useful for softening available or strobe light at home, in the studio, and on location. There are many different types of diffusion screen fabrics, which provide different qualities and colors of light. I find the most useful size to be 3½×6½-foot because these can be used for full-length or head shots. Lightweight frames are available to hold the fabric, and they fold down into compact, easy-to-carry units. Purchase these from mail-order photographic suppliers and local retailers, or make your own diffusion screen by draping an ordinary white sheet between two light stands.

• **Gobos** create the opposite effect of reflectors. Rather than bouncing light, they absorb it to create shadowed areas and block light from spilling. Make your own gobos from black tagboard or black velvet-like fabric. To use, position gobos just outside the frame opposite whatever subject or surface you wish to remain shadowed.

• **Diffusers** can be mounted over the lens to soften skin texture, contrast and shadows, and create an interesting "flare" effect on white areas in a picture. Tiffen brand diffusers provide the slightest diffusion. Tiffen #1 is my favorite in diffusers for photographing children, because it softens skin texture without lowering contrast or changing the exposure of a picture. The #3 is a good choice, as well. Softar diffusers, made by Hasselblad, are also fairly good, though they do lower contrast. Use the Softar #1. The #2 creates a somewhat "mushy" look.

Many photographers like to create their own diffusers. Start with a small square of Plexiglas or glass, and apply hair spray, Vaseline or nail polish to the areas you wish to diffuse, or stretch a fine net or panty hose over your lens. *Caution*: If you use nail polish, be sure it's dry before getting it near your lens. If you get Vaseline on your lens, carefully clean it off with lens cleaning solution.

• **Lens-mounted color conversion filters** made of gelatin or polyester change all color wavelengths and can be used to alter the color balance of a photograph. Usually, in photographing children, color conversion filters are used to warm the overall effect. I frequently use Kodak 8 1EF on overcast days, in north light, or when I want a sentimental or old-fashioned look.

LIGHT AND MODIFIER STANDS, ETC. Unless you hand hold your strobe, to use any light source with or without a modifier, you need a stand for holding these components. The best and most portable light and reflector stands are made of lightweight aluminum because of the ease in carrying and transporting them. I use Bogen stands. Photographers breaking into child portraiture should consider buying at least three stands, so you can use up to three light heads at one time. Sizes and costs vary. Another important piece of equipment is an 18 percent gray card. You need an 18 percent gray card, which equates to a medium tone, for through-the-lens metering indoors or outdoors, so the meter isn't fooled by the intensity of a very light or very dark element in your portrait. These are inexpensive and are available at your local photo store.

PREPARE A SITE KIT Every photographer should have a site kit that contains a first aid kit, a Swiss army knife, black electrical tape, photographer's tape, string, a Nerf ball, a squeaky toy, processing envelopes for the photolab, hairpins, safety pins, a cloth diaper, and a bandana. Every item has come in handy at one time or another for various purposes, both in the studio and on location.

WHERE TO BUY EQUIPMENT New York mail-order retailers advertise in photographic magazines offering "gray market" merchandise. This usually is the same name brand equipment you purchase from regular retailers, but is imported from Europe and Japan and often comes without an American warranty. The prices can be as much as 20 percent lower than equipment available from American retailers. If you're a bit of a gambler and think you can live without a warranty, you might try buying on the gray market.

Mail-order retailers that offer merchandise with American warranties often, but not always, offer prices up to 10 percent below those offered at retail stores. You can also buy used equipment very economically by mail order. This is a good option for amateurs, although used equipment comes without a warranty.

Local retailers either stock or can order almost any piece of equipment you need. Shop around to find the best price. Often, they'll reduce a price to meet or beat a competitor or throw in extras like film or additional equipment, especially on high-ticket items.

Used rental equipment is usually available in metropolitan areas. When equipment becomes outdated or for some reason becomes unrentable (but not unusable) businesses often offer it for sale at excellent prices. Don't expect to read about this kind of deal in the classifieds. Most of it is snapped up by photographers who hear about it through the grapevine before word trickles down to the general public. So contact rental shops and let them know what you're looking for. Ask if they have a waiting list, and get your name on it.

SHOPPING FOR USED EQUIPMENT

Other used equipment can be found at professional photographers' retirement and going-out-of-business sales. Check the bulletin boards at commercial labs and photo rental shops. Watch the classifieds looking for swap meets where you can shop the offerings of many photographers and dealers at once. Often, you can get better prices if you purchase an entire package (camera body, lenses, film backs, etc.), rather than individual pieces.

THE ADVANTAGES OF RENTING

If there's a piece of equipment you're dying to try, here are five good reasons to rent before you own:

1. You're not sure if it'll work out for you.
2. You're comparison shopping and you want to get the feel for several different brands of lights or cameras before you make the big plunge.
3. You're shooting out of town and don't want to haul several tons of gear on the plane.
4. You have infrequent need for expensive equipment for special jobs or self-assignment.
5. You're getting more interested in photography and want to explore the medium without spending a lot of money.

Learn the ropes of renting photographic equipment. Rental prices and selection can vary from place to place, so shop around. As a renter, you're liable for damage to any equipment you receive, so check it out before you leave the store to see that it's all in working order. If the equipment becomes damaged while in your possession, you'll be charged for its repair or replacement. The staff at many photographic rental stores are often photographers and may be able to advise you about appropriate equipment for portraiture.

Sure, renting is inconvenient. You have to call in your order, pick it up, drop it off, sometimes what you want isn't available, and you don't get the thrill of owning. But sometimes renting is the only logical solution. If you do decide to rent, here's what you should do to see that your needs are met:

• Be explicit when you phone in to reserve your equipment. Tell them exactly what you need.

• Develop a relationship with more than one rental shop in your city, so that if one doesn't have something you need, you can try another.

• Check all the equipment at the rental shop when you pick it up to see that it's all there and all in working order.

The relatively high speed of Kodak Tri-X 400 professional film allowed me to capture this humorous and
joyful moment. Because of the archival properties of
black-and-white film, this boy's children will be able to
enjoy this picture—and perhaps even their children.

Indoors; available light; Nikon 8008; Nikkor 180mm AF lens; Kodak Tri-X 400 (b&w professional film).

There are a bazillion different types of film to choose from, not to mention papers to
print on, and processing chemicals that alter the look of the film and photos. Test
shoot as many different film types as you can afford. Then pick the films that give you
the look you love and stick to them. Use the film to help shape your personal style
and your approach to a given photo session. For instance, if you have low light and
a small format camera, don't go for the moderate grain of a 400 ISO film: go all the
way with a fast, high-grained film of 1000 or even 1600 ISO. If it's a sharp image you
want, use a slow film of 25 to 100 ISO and a medium format camera. (ISO is a guide
to the amount of light required to make a normal exposure on a particular film. The
higher the ISO rating the less light the film requires.)

PROFESSIONAL FILMS

There are several major differences between so-called professional films and amateur
films. Amateur films have a long shelf life and do not require refrigeration. Professional
films require refrigeration and have a shorter shelf life, because they are manufactured
to more exacting standards and uniformity of emulsions. Often, high-volume shooters
purchase entire film lots to insure exactly predictable results from job to job and store
them in their freezers. Professional film is available in all formats and speeds, and in
print and chrome varieties.

To buy professional film, look in your Yellow Pages under photographic supplies/
equipment for photographic retailers. Wholesale labs and professional labs also carry
professional photographic materials and films, but their stock may be more limited.

Many of the roll films listed below are available in sheet film sizes 4×5, 5×7,
8×10 and 11×14.

COLOR PRINT FILM

Most amateur and professional portrait photographers shoot 35mm and 70mm print
film, rather than chrome (slide) film. It is easier and less expensive to make enlargements, and the results are generally better. Color print film is available from 25 to
1600 ISO. Color balance, color saturation and exposure latitude vary significantly from
type to type. Brands of print film include:

Vericolor III professional (VPS) (Kodak)

- ISO 160
- Excellent exposure latitude: we've gotten great results from 2 stops underexposed to 3 stops over.
- Ideal for shooting kids: beautiful skin tones, realistic color reproduction, medium contrast, and broad exposure latitude make this the most popular film among professional portrait photographers. I recommend it for amateurs, as well.

Reala professional (Fuji)

- ISO 100
- Excellent exposure latitude, similar to Kodak's VPS.
- Excellent for shooting kids: similar to, but with slightly more vibrance, than VPS.
- Special characteristic: Reala compensates for, or neutralizes, light with different color balances in all color hues. Where fluorescent light appears green and tungsten light yellow on other film, they all come out virtually correct—natural looking—on Reala.

Kodacolor Gold Plus amateur (Kodak)

- ISO 100, 200, 400, 1600
- Excellent exposure latitude.
- Good film for general photography: skin tones aren't quite as good as with VPS or Reala; tends to be a little contrasty.
- Since this is an amateur film, it can be purchased at many one-hour photo stores and drugstores.

Ektapress Gold (Kodak)

- ISO 100, 400, 1600
- Seems to have a more limited exposure latitude than the film above.
- Ektapress 1600 is the best high-speed film we've tried. A must for shooting kids in extremely low light situations. It's on the contrasty side, though not bad for such a high-speed film. Unlike Fuji's Reala, it doesn't correct or neutralize color balance, so if you're shooting with tungsten light, you'll want to use an over-the-lens color correction filter (see chapter 8 for more on color correction filters).
- Special characteristics: although this film has professional characteristics, it doesn't need to be refrigerated, so you can stash a few rolls in your camera bag to have available all the time; available only in propacks of five thirty-six exposure rolls, and press packs of fifty thirty-six exposure rolls; ideally you should have ISO 1600 film processed and printed at a commercial lab—one-hour photo stores in my experience sometimes make contrasty, overly dark, off-color prints.

Ektar (Kodak)

- ISO 25, 100, 1000
- Somewhat limited exposure latitude.
- Ektar 25 provides amazingly fine grain and beautiful color, but its limited exposure latitude makes it less handy for photographing kids (in contrasty or unpredictable lighting situations, you may want to bracket); select this film over Vericolor III or Reala if you require extremely fine grain for enlargements, or serious color saturation.

Fuji professional and amateur

- ISO 400
- Average exposure latitude.
- This is the best medium speed film we've found for shooting kids, very fine grain for its speed, and soft tones make it ideal for portraiture.

COLOR CHROME FILM

35mm chrome (also called slide or transparency film) is used most often by commercial stock photographers whose work is to be reproduced using color separation rather than photographic processes. It can be a good choice for photographing children, because processing is adjustable to compensate for incorrect exposure, which is not possible with print film. General exposure latitude, however, is much more limited than with print film. If you do shoot chrome film with the intention of making prints or enlargements, read about the two types of printing methods in chapter 10.

Velvia professional (Fuji)

- ISO 50
- The best skin tones of any chrome film, hands down; excellent color saturation; great detail and contrast; virtually no grain structure; almost a three-dimensional quality.
- Special characteristics: while Fuji rates Velvia at ISO 50, in my own experience it's closer to 25.

Fujichrome professional and amateur (Fuji)

- ISO 50, 64T, 100, 400, 1600
- Fujichrome is my favorite 400 ISO chrome film for photographing kids. Good skin tones, contrast, detail and color saturation in the full range of speeds.

Ektachrome amateur and professional (Kodak)

- ISO 50HC, 64, 100, 160, 200, 400, 800
- I personally dislike Ektachrome for photographing kids. I think it gives unattractive skin tones and an overall cool color balance. In north light on overcast days

or in open shade, it looks positively blue unless you use a lot of color corrective filters. But I have friends who do excellent work and swear by it. Test it yourself to see if you like it.

• Kodak has recently introduced two new films, Ektachrome 64X and 100X, which it advertises as having a warmer tone and finer grain than the old Ektachrome, but I have no experience with these.

Kodachrome professional and amateur (Kodak)

• ISO 25, 40, 64, 200

• Warmer skin tones than Ektachrome, little grain, very high color saturation.

• Special characteristics: unlike other chrome films, which are developed using the E-6 process, Kodachrome must be developed using the K-14 process, which is available at only a few labs in the country. You can purchase prepaid mailers to send your Kodachrome to a K-14 lab, or bring it to your regular commercial processor and they'll mail it for you.

Scotch 1000 professional (3M)

• ISO 1000

• This chrome film has a beautiful, high-grained but even texture, so it gives a crisper look than any other high-grained film. Shoot and process normally, or shoot at ISO 2000 and ask your lab to push process 1 stop.

• Special characteristics: like many fast films, it has a slightly cool, or blue, color balance. Shoot with an 8 1EF color corrective filter. When you first begin to shoot Scotch 1000, ask your lab to do clip tests (processing only a few frames from the roll so the balance can be adjusted accordingly) until you can get a feel for the exposure you prefer. Rewind this film manually (slowly) to avoid blue and white static spots down the center of the film.

BLACK-AND-WHITE FILM

Just as with direct color photography, there are many different film types.

Tri-X pan professional (Kodak)

• ISO 400

• Great exposure latitude, often used by photojournalists; a versatile film, fast enough for use in most lighting situations; fairly high grain, high contrast; good for push processing for a high contrast, impressionistic look.

Plus-X pan professional (Kodak)

• ISO 125

• Good exposure latitude; fine grain, good sharpness; good for use in studio or outdoors.

Tmax 100 professional (Kodak)

- ISO 100
- Can be adjusted in processing without harming overall quality, nearly grainless, fantastic detail and sharpness, the black-and-white film of choice in studios.

Tmax 400 professional (Kodak)

- ISO 400
- The same speed as Tri-X, but noticeably finer grained; like Tmax 100, can be adjusted in processing without damaging quality.

Tmax P3200 professional (Kodak)

- ISO 3200 (can also be shot at 6400)
- Fast film with fantastic exposure latitude and grain comparable to Tri-X that has been pushed 1 1/2 stops; great for shooting in low light situations.

Technical pan professional (Kodak)

- ISO 25
- Virtually grainless; high resolution; can give interesting, nearly white skin tone; great detail can be maintained even in high contrast printing.

FILM TO ALWAYS HAVE ON HAND

Don't fall into the trap of simply having a few rolls of ISO 400 amateur film laying around. It may work, but your results won't be extraordinary. This is what I like to keep in my freezer and/or camera bag:

- *Kodak VPS* or *Fuji Reala* for situations when there's plenty of light such as outdoors in full sun or with electronic flash.
- *Fuji 400 professional* for moderate to low lighting situations such as indoors when you want to avoid using electronic flash.
- *Kodak Ektapress 1600* for use in very low light such as a birthday party in a darkened room illuminated by candlelight from the cake.
- *Fuji Velvia* for well-lit situations when a positive (chrome) image is desired.
- *Fujichrome ISO 100* and *ISO 400* for moderate to well-lit scenes indoors and out.
- *3M Scotch 1000* for use in low light and to combine with push processing for highly grained, impressionistic images.
- *Kodak Tmax 100* for fine-grained black-and-white images of well-lit scenes.
- *Kodak Tmax 400* for reasonably fine-grained black-and-white images in moderate to low light.
- *Kodak Tri-X* for use in combination with push processing for highly grained images in low light.

Quality, handline processing and hand-printing of this picture give it the beautiful white highlights, black blacks and detail throughout the entire tonal range, which is the sign of a successful black-and-white portrait.

Strobes; studio; Nikon 8008; Nikkor 35-105mm zoom AF lens; Kodak Plus-X 100 (b&w professional film).

If you're an amateur, you're probably used to using the one-hour photo lab for processing, enlargements, and even purchasing your film. There's no doubt these places are convenient, and they serve a valuable purpose. But there are professional (also called commercial) labs that welcome the general public and can open up a whole new world of creative and technical control to you. In many cases, processing and proofing at these labs is not more expensive than at the one-hour places. Let's look at the features of and differences in the three types of labs—one-hour, commercial and wholesale.

ONE-HOUR LABS

- *Processing* is of 35mm only. They are economical and fast. Usually only one type of chemistry is available.
- *Printing* is standard 3½ × 5 and 4 × 6 prints; glossy or matte. Usually only one brand of paper is available.
- *Enlargements* are machine prints, in standard sizes to 20 × 30. Some places now offer custom cropping for an additional charge.
- *Processing and printing of black-and-white film* is available at most national chains. Usually only one type of chemistry and one type of glossy resin-coated paper is available.
- *Chrome services* include E-6 processing and mounting, and either type "r" or type "c" prints. Some places will sell you the internegatives from type "c" prints. See page 96 for an explanation of "r" and "c" prints.
- *Other services and merchandise* at some national chains includes copy stand work (photographic copies of flat artwork or photographs), in-store credit cards, credit on merchandise returns, professional and volume discounts, photo novelties such as Christmas ornaments and photo sculptures, ready-made frames, mats and photo cubes and photo greeting cards.

COMMERCIAL/ PROFESSIONAL LABS

- *Processing* is of all film types. Custom hand processing is available at an additional charge as are different chemistries, clip tests and adjusted processing.
- *Proofing* materials are standard 3½ × 5 and 4 × 6 glossy or matte finish machine

prints, contact sheets, numbered proofs on medium and large format film and chromes, and enlarged (11×14 and 16×20) proof sheets.

- *Printing* is machine and custom, and can include cropping, burning (making certain areas of a print darker), and dodging (making certain areas of a print lighter). Any size print is available to 46×96. Cibachrome prints, and borderless, black-bordered, or white-bordered prints are also available.

- *Complete black-and-white services* are available including prints made on fiber-base paper, sepia toning, selenium toning and composites.

- *Complete chrome services* are available including internegatives up to 8×10 for making prints, duplicating, type "r" and type "c" prints, and poster size transparencies.

- *Other services and merchandise* include retouching and airbrushing, color laser and bubble-jet copies, kodalith, pickup and delivery, overtime and rush service, store credit cards, professional and volume discounts, copy stand, masking, contrast control masking, retouching, digital imaging, and professional film and supplies.

WHOLESALE LABS

Wholesale labs cater to professional photographers and specialize in portraiture and wedding photography. You must be a professional photographer and have a tax-exempt number to patronize a wholesale lab.

- *Processing* is available for all film types. Adjusted processing may or may not be available.

- *Proofing materials* include numbered negatives and proofs, enlarged proofs, contact sheets, projection proofs.

- *Printing* is computer analyzed machine prints (also called auto prints), and custom printing with cropping, burning and dodging. Other services include enlargements up to 20×30 and sometimes larger, studio name embossed on prints, economical portrait packages from the same or multiple negatives, burning in of edges, and diffusion (softening the focus and contrast of the image).

- *Black-and-white services* include standard processing and printing on resin-coated, glossy paper. Black-and-white prints are available from Kodak VPS III color negatives.

- *Chrome service* is E-6 processing (adjusted processing not always available), mounting, 35mm chromes from 35mm negatives (projection proofs), machine and custom type "c" prints, internegatives (may only be available in the same size as the original chrome).

- *Other services and merchandise* include lab credit cards, volume discounts,

retouching and airbrushing, proof albums, photo albums, professional film and supplies, photo folders.

To get the best product at the least expense from your lab:

• Shop around for the best quality and the best price. Prices can vary significantly, even from one professional lab to another. But don't sacrifice quality for low cost.

• Ask questions. Develop an understanding of what your lab actually can do for you, and what is simply impossible.

• Learn the lingo. For instance, *format* refers to the size, shape and proportion of film. 35mm film is small format; 70mm film is medium format; 4 × 5 and 8 × 10 sheet film is large format. Another example: *reciprocity effect* is when a film is exposed for a longer or shorter time than it was designed for. Color balance is distorted and may need to be corrected.

• Learn what each lab does best and use them for their specialty. I use four different labs: one for black-and-white processing and proofing and type "r" prints from color chromes, one for color processing and proofing and color printing from print film, one for chrome processing and type "c" prints, and one for the rare occasions when I send out black-and-white custom printing.

• Most labs guarantee their work. There's not much you can do if your printing gets ruined (and even the best labs mess up once in a while and most only replace the destroyed film), but if you get unsatisfactory proofs or enlargements, send them back and ask them to do it again. They should be happy to comply.

The processing of chrome film and some black-and-white print films (such as Fuji Velvia 100 and Kodak Tri-X 400) can be adjusted to compensate for over or underexposure. If you're uncertain about your exposure, you can bring your film to a professional lab and ask for a clip test. They will process only the first two or three shots on the roll for you to examine. Then the processing of the balance can be adjusted to make the final product darker or lighter, as necessary. *Pushing*, or overprocessing the film brightens and lightens it, in some cases causing greater contrast, color saturation, and higher grain. *Holding*, or underprocessing, darkens the finished product, in some cases lowering contrast and muddying colors. While adjusting the processing, especially within the range of ¼ to 1 stop, can improve the results when film is exposed incorrectly, it cannot completely undo the damage—overexposed film will still lose detail in the highlights, and underexposed film will still lose detail in the shadows. Some films that respond well to push processing are Velvia (pushing less than 1 stop won't damage the quality) and 3M Scotch 1000 (see chapter 9 for more details on these and other film types).

Think of your negative or chrome as raw material, not as a finished product. There is no one correct way to print any given photo: give the same negative to 100 different people to print, and you'll wind up with 100 different pictures. The more you understand about what results are possible from color printing, and the more explicit you can be about what you want, the better your color lab can please you.

Contrast is critical and balancing it can be tricky, since what constitutes good or bad contrast is partly subjective. Too little contrast and a print looks flat, lifeless, colorless and one dimensional. Too much contrast, and colors look artificial, shadows block up (muddy up and lose detail), and highlights blow out (go too light with little or no detail). Make sure your color prints have white whites, black blacks, and good detail in both highlights and shadows. Contrast can be adjusted somewhat in the color printing process, but not to the degree that it can be in black-and-white printing.

Color balance is critical, too. All color prints have yellow, magenta (a red), and cyan (a bluish-green) in them. If your print looks too blue or too green (cool), it needs less cyan. If it appears too pink or purple, request less magenta, or less cyan and magenta. If it appears too yellow, it of course needs less yellow. Too much cyan, in addition to cooling the tone of a print, makes it more contrasty, as well. Too much yellow lowers the contrast and muddies the blue tones.

Uniformly poor color balance in a negative or chrome film, such as the blue cast caused by shooting under an overcast sky, can be partly or even completely corrected in the printing process. Irregular areas of poor color such as those caused by multiple light types, are not nearly as correctable.

Density refers to the darkness or lightness of a print. If you think the print is too light, you need to ask for more density; too dark, it needs less density. Prints made from negatives and chromes that are too dark or too light can be partially and sometimes completely corrected.

Use a proof, or 4×6 print, as a jumping-off place for your lab when requesting reprints. Mark cropping instructions right on the face of the proof. Indicate whether you want your enlargement to have the same contrast, color balance and density as the proof, or whether you want it darker, lighter, warmer or cooler.

In addition to adjusting contrast, color balance and overall density, your print can be custom cropped (printing only a portion of the image), burned (darkening areas of a print), dodged (lightening areas of a print), vignetted (burning in the edges of the shot) and diffused (softening the focus and contrast).

Two types of prints can be made from chrome film. Type "r" prints are made directly from the original, positive image and are crisper and clearer than type "c." They are also less expensive but can be more contrasty and hold less detail. Many commercial printers discourage customers from using type "r," and some simply don't offer it.

Type "c" prints are made from an internegative: a negative image that is made from the original, positive image. Because this process involves an extra step, or generation, the enlargements can appear slightly fuzzy. But the larger the internegative, the crisper the picture. "Interneg" sizes commonly made from 35mm chromes are 35mm, 6.7 and 4×5. For most enlargement sizes it's not necessary to make an internegative larger than 4×5.

Most one-hour photo stores offer either type "r" or type "c" from 35mm internegatives, but usually not both. Ask which they use.

**PROCESSING
BLACK-AND-
WHITE
PICTURES**

Black and white is considered by many to be the ultimate photographic portrait medium. With archival processing and professional framing, black-and-white photographs will survive from generation to generation. The simplicity and drama of black and white makes pictures that can be ageless, nostalgic or contemporary. When it's used in photographing a child, I think the subject's personality, character and spirit are represented more truly and clearly in black and white than in color, which can compete with and distract from the subject.

Where to go for processing. Though the one-hour photo labs will take black-and-white processing, I don't recommend using them. They receive them so infrequently I can't believe their chemistry is always fresh, they don't offer adjusted processing, and they usually only have one type of chemistry.

Find at least two different professional processors. Shoot two short "test" rolls of your favorite film, with exactly the same subject and lighting. Send one to each lab for processing, then have contact sheets printed at normal (#2) contrast. Look for noticeable differences in quality of grain, contrast and density.

I once made the mistake of assuming that professional labs all ran black-and-white film for processing in the chemistry recommended by the film manufacturer—I was wrong. I had switched from one professional lab to another for processing, and suddenly found that when I printed my pictures there was noticeably higher contrast and slightly more grain than before. Nothing about our shooting had changed. I finally called my new processor, and discovered that they were running my Kodak Plus-X pan professional film in Tmax film chemistry.

Of course, you can always process your black-and-white film yourself, for ultimate control. Find a book that describes the black-and-white processing methods.

How to recognize good black-and-white prints. To evaluate a black-and-white print, look for these qualities: The blacks should be solidly black, and the whites should be white. Look at the pupils—that's the one area of every print that should be true black. The skin tones should be pleasing, not muddy. The face should appear softly contoured, not flat. There should be good detail in the complete tonal range.

Unlike direct color photography, which can often be successfully printed by machine, black-and-white machine prints are rarely of really good quality. It requires a human touch and a discerning eye to achieve pleasing skin tones and overall contrast, and it's a rare negative that doesn't require some custom dodging or burning.

If possible, find a professional lab that specializes in custom black-and-white printing. Always ask for archival paper and processing to guarantee that in fifty years, your children's children will be able to enjoy the portraits you make today.

Really good custom archival black-and-white printing is hard to find, and costly. Consider setting up your own darkroom in your basement or extra bathroom. If you want to do your own black-and-white printing, but aren't able to set up your own darkroom, look into these alternatives:

• Photographic equipment rental shops often also rent darkroom time; you supply your own chemistry.

• Universities and community education programs frequently offer adult extension courses in photography, which allow you access to their darkrooms. In situations like these, check the chemistry to see that it's fresh.

• Other photographers are sometimes willing to rent their darkrooms. Put up a note on the bulletin board at your professional processing lab.

PHOTO RETOUCHING

Retouching is generally only available at professional and wholesale labs. The charge is figured either by the head (subject) or by the hour, with a fifteen minute minimum.

Retouching on negatives can correct blemishes, wrinkles, and shadows cast on the face, such as by eyeglasses. Some labs will only add density to an area on the negative, making it appear lighter in the finished print. Other labs may also offer retouching techniques that subtract density on certain areas of the negative, making it appear darker on the finished print. In addition, retouching can open eyes; remove red eye, moles, and wrinkles; and replace missing teeth.

AVAILABLE LIGHT

This shot was made with available light from a north-facing window in the afternoon.

Equipment:
Nikon FE2 camera body, 35 to 105mm zoom lens, tripod.
Materials:
Kodak Tri-X professional film.
Procedure:
• Position your subject approximately 5 feet from the window at a 45 degree angle; 5 feet in front of the camera; background or backdrop 12 feet behind your subject. White fill card as close to the subject as possible (usually about 18 inches) on the side opposite the window, also at a 45 degree angle.
• Shoot at ISO 800, overexposing 2 stops from average meter reading.
• Push process 1½ stops.
• Print made on Kodak Polyfiber glossy paper, with a 2½ contrast filter.

This shot was made in the studio using strobe light and reflectors. If you don't have strobes, you can substitute an electronic flash unit on an extension cord held away from the camera. Position your subject at least five feet away from a white wall, so the wall will appear dark relative to the subject, approximating the backdrop in the illustration.

Equipment:
Nikon 8008, 35 to 105mm zoom, strobe unit, two light heads, two soft boxes, two white fill cards.

Materials:
Kodak Plus-X professional film, ISO 125.

Procedure:
• Position your subject, reflector, and background the same as for the "Available Light" project, but use a strobe inside a soft box instead of window light.
• Expose film at 1½ stops over average meter reading.
• Process normal.
• Print on graded Agfa Portriga 118, matte finish, contrast 2.

Special Notes:
Even with the light hitting the subject at almost the same angle, an available light shot has a softer look; the strobe shot has a more sparkling appearance.

The photographic techniques included in this chapter for you to re-create range from the very simple to the very difficult. One requires only an open shade and a kid. On the other end of the spectrum, some require special papers, photo oils, and other materials and equipment. But the more complicated techniques don't necessarily yield more creative or beautiful results. In the hands of a skilled, intuitive photographer, the most straightforward techniques can make the most timeless, successful portraits.

In some cases I've listed alternative equipment and materials, so don't be shy about using substitutes if you don't have, for instance, a 180mm lens, or if you want to put your own personal spin on the projects. Note, too, that guidelines for setting up your camera, subject and background relative to one another are only suggestions. The distance between the camera and the subject, and the subject and the background, will vary depending on focal length and personal preference for cropping.

Tackle whatever techniques appeal to your curiosity and ability level. And even if you're advanced enough to complete the difficult ones, don't shun the simple ones. They may help you create your most memorable pictures.

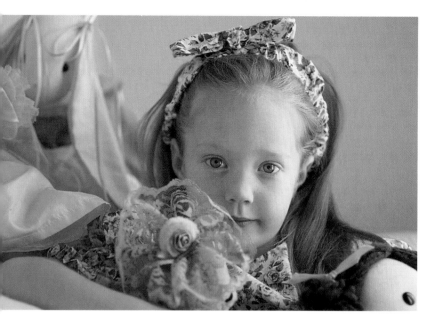

DIFFUSION SCREENS

This picture was made in the subject's bedroom amid her collection of dolls. The light came from the east-facing window late in the morning. There was just barely enough light to shoot at a thirtieth of a second at f2.8—a lighting situation in which most photographers would resort to electronic flash or a faster film. While flash would have made an acceptable picture, the fine grain and soft shadow play would have been lost, along with the beautiful mood of this shot.

Equipment:
Nikon 8008; 180mm lens; two 4 × 8 diffusion screens.
Materials:
Velvia chrome film, ASA 50.
Procedure:
• Position your subject about 5 feet from the window at a 90 degree angle; 10 feet in front of the camera; wall 2 feet behind the subject; diffusion screens on either side of the subject within approximately 2 feet.
• Shoot 1⅓ stops open from the through-the-lens or average spot meter reading.
• Process film normally.
Special Notes:
Because the picture was made during the morning with light from an east-facing window, the sun was pounding straight in, necessitating diffusion screens. Had the picture been made later in the day, the sun would have been in a different position, and the shot could have been made without the screens.
Alternative Equipment and Materials:
Equally satisfactory results can be achieved using print film, from which it is easier and less expensive to make enlarged prints. Kodak VPS III professional film or Fuji Reala are good choices.

A SIMPLE SHOT

This shot was made on a sunny afternoon in open shade with no flash and no reflectors. It goes to prove that it doesn't take a lot of fancy equipment, exotic light, or lots of styling and "stuff" to make a great picture: all you really need is a kid.

Equipment:
Nikon 8008; 180mm lens.
Materials:
Kodak Ektar 125 print film.
Procedure:
• Position yourself and your subject in any orientation within open shade.
• Shoot film on average meter reading.
• Process film normally.
Special Notes:
Kodak Ektar 125 has a more limited exposure range than VPS III, so you may want to bracket if you feel uncertain of your metering.
Alternative Equipment and Materials:
You can substitute Kodak VPS III or Fuji Reala for warmer color balance and greater exposure latitude.

SIMPLE HAND-COLORING

(Left.) You don't have to make a big investment to explore hand-coloring techniques. This picture was made by photocopying a black-and-white photographic print, and coloring the copy with colored markers, highlighter pens and colored pencils.

Equipment:
Photocopier.
Materials:
Black-and-white or color photograph; colored markers, highlighters, colored pencils.
Procedure:
• Make photocopies of original pictures.
• Color with markers, highlighters or pencils.

SERIOUS HAND-COLORING

(Right.) If you're interested in getting more serious about hand-coloring photographs, and you want to explore the use of oil paints and archival paper, here's my technique.

Equipment:
None.
Materials:
An 8 × 10 print on black-and-white, matte finish, fiberbase paper, printed at slightly lower contrast and slightly lighter than a normal black-and-white print (I use Agfa Portriga 118 matte paper); Marshall photo oils and colored pencils; Prismacolor pencils; cotton balls and cotton swabs; kneaded rubber eraser.
Procedure:
• Apply white and carmine photo oils, mixed in equal parts lightly on the background with cotton balls. Apply this color slightly into the figures too, to create a smooth transition between the background and the figures.
• Now remove the background color that you blended into the figures with a kneaded rubber eraser.
• Let the background dry about three days before applying the clothing colors. The colors of the girl's stripes are Marshall pencils orchid and sky blue; the sunglasses and bracelet are cadmium yellow and viridian green. The boy's coveralls are Prismacolor true blue, the buttons and hardware Prismacolor raw sienna; his shirt stripes are Prismacolor aquamarine. Skin tones are Marshall basic flesh mixed with a *tiny* bit of serge blue. Lips are the Marshall pencil called cheek; cheeks are Marshall oil paint color called cheek. Hair is Marshall oil color sepia extra strong.

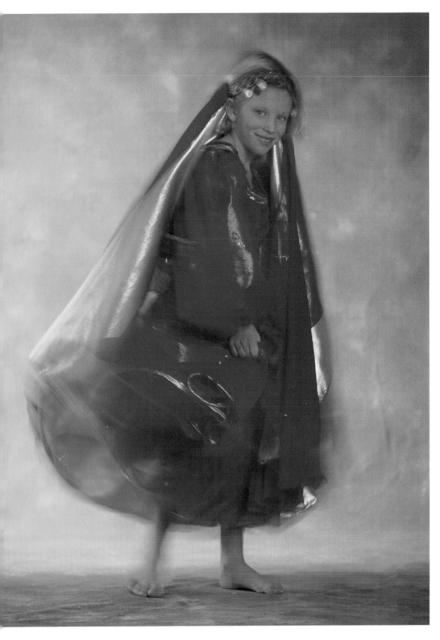

GHOSTING

This technique uses a relatively long exposure during which tungsten light illuminates the backdrop and strobe light illuminates the subject. The longer tungsten exposure following the 250th second strobe blast allows you to convey movement by showing a "ghost" of your subject blurred against the background.

Equipment:
Small or medium format camera, medium length lens, tripod, tungsten light, strobe unit with one light head, soft box, umbrella or bare head reflector.
Materials:
Any relatively slow chrome or negative film.
Procedure:
• Position your subject at least 10 feet from your backdrop; position your light sources at whatever distance necessary to achieve the desired meter reading.
• The tungsten light on the backdrop should read on your meter about ½ stop darker than the strobe light on the subject.
• Shoot at a range of shutter speeds, from 1/8th to 1/30th. The amount of blurring you get will vary depending on how fast the subject is moving and the shutter speed.
Special Notes:
Since it's impossible to predict your results, shoot many shots at each shutter speed. Because you'll be asking your subject to repeat her movement many times, it's important to work with an older child who's enthusiastic about helping to make the picture. If you have trouble getting the strobe and tungsten lights within ½ stop of one another because the strobes are too strong and the tungsten is too weak, try putting all your spare light heads onto your power box and firing them in the wrong direction to drain off power.

INDIRECT FLASH

This shot was made indoors with electronic flash bounced off a wall. Bouncing the flash creates a much softer, more natural look than direct flash.

Equipment:
Nikon 8008, 180mm lens, #3 Tiffen diffuser for over-the-lens, electronic flash unit.
Materials:
Fujichrome 100 professional film, Tiffen #3 soft focus filter.
Procedure:
• Position your subject approximately 6 feet in front of the camera; background should be at least six feet away to avoid unwanted shadows; direct the flash at a wall that is at a 45 to 90 degree angle to your subject.
• Expose film ½ stop open from meter reading.
• Point camera-mounted flash at the wall at an angle to bounce onto the subject.
Special Notes:
It's important to position the flash in relation to the reflector, in this case the wall, in an optimal position for lighting the subject. Remember that the angle of incidence is equal to the angle of reflection. You may want to practice your aim using some test rolls before using this technique on an important subject.
Alternative Equipment and Materials:
Rather than a wall, a white reflector card can be substituted. Comparable print films are VPS III and Fuji Reala.

COOKIES

By using a hard, focused light and putting cutouts of various shapes (called cookies) in between the light source and the subject, you can cast shadow patterns that simulate naturally occurring patterns caused by light passing through windows, trees, reflecting off water and others. Cookies and mounts for tungsten lights can be purchased through theatrical supply companies, but you can make your own from cardboard that suit your needs more precisely and for practically no money. For this shot, we made a cookie that simulated window light with 2-inch × 4-foot strips of cardboard that we taped together while our models were changing clothes.

Equipment:
Nikon 8008, Nikkor 180/2.8 AF lens, tungsten theatrical spotlight, two white reflector cards, six 2-inch × 4-foot strips of cardboard, tape.

Materials:
Kodachrome 200 professional film.

Procedure:
• Position your subject approximately 12 feet from the light source, at a 45 degree angle from both the camera and the light source. Move your cookie back and forth. The closer the cookie is to the light source, the more diffused the shadow pattern will be; the closer the cookie is to the subject, the harder the shadow pattern will be.

• Expose film at 1 stop open from the average meter reading.

• Process film normally.

Asking the kids simple questions can elicit fun expressions. This little girl looks coy because I just asked her the name of her cat.

Strobe; studio; Nikon 8008; Nikkor 35-105mm zoom AF lens; Kodak Plus-X 100 (professional film); printed on Agfa Portriga 118 #2 contrast paper; hand-colored with artist's oils and colored pencils.

If you're a parent, you probably could have written this chapter yourself. You can skip forward to read about posing kids, or you might want to browse this section just to affirm your experience in working with kids.

There is a myth surrounding child photography that it is somehow difficult—sometimes even impossible—to work with kids. When I announced to my photographer friends my intentions of channeling my energies into child portraiture, I was met with sarcasm and astonishment. Comments such as, *Why would you want to do that? Kids will really make you sing for your supper!* abounded. And my friends were not the only ones who held this opinion. A nationally published photography trade publication ran an article in 1991 that purported to help photographers make portraits of "... your most challenging subjects," and went on to state, "... professional photographers dread working with youngsters ... they [kids] care more about having fun than creating a great portrait."

Well, I'm here to tell you that if it isn't fun to make a great children's portrait (for both the photographer and the subject), then the portrait simply won't be great. And contrary to popular belief, children are perhaps the *easiest* subjects I've ever photographed. That's not to say that shooting kids isn't hard work—it is. But what worthwhile pursuit isn't?

Photographers run into trouble in working with children when they try to make them behave like little adults. If you let a kid be a kid, you can't help but get excellent results. I recall one client who came to me after being terribly disappointed with another photographer's work on her daughter's age two portrait. Trying to describe to me over the phone what she didn't like about it, she said, "She's a beautiful, vibrant little girl, but this picture is so ... stiff. She looks like she's thirty years old. He made a sow's ear from a silk purse!"

I try to capture natural movements in my work—not just action, but those totally unself-conscious attitudes. The little girl playing with the fringe on her dress or playing with her hair; the little boy standing on the sides of his feet or twisting his sweater into knots; the kids playing air guitar or acting out exactly how the little engine that could made it up that steep hill. When people see my work for the first time they

There is a myth that kids are somehow harder to photograph than adults. I find kids to be the easiest and most rewarding subjects. How many adults would have as much fun or look as natural in a portrait as this girl?

Strobe; studio; Nikon 8008; Nikkor 35-105mm zoom AF lens; Kodak Plus-X 100 (professional film); printed on Agfa Portriga 118 #2 contrast paper; hand-colored with Marshall photo oils and colored pencils.

often ask me, *How did you get them to do that?* My question to them is, *How would I get them to stop?*

There are no tricks to making children behave like children. There is an art, however, to earning a child's trust and helping her true personality and spirit shine through. And while children, like adults, are all individuals who respond to different things, there are certain constants, which I call Vik's Ten Commandments. If you learn them, you can take the myth of the difficult child subject and turn it into the magic of a great photograph.

VIK'S TEN
COMMANDMENTS

1. Thou shalt not say "smile."

There are literally hundreds of facial muscles involved in a smile. It's nearly impossible for children or adults to give a natural smile on command. Instead of telling them to smile, give them a reason to. Make them really feel like smiling, and they will. One of the surest ways to get a child to smile at you is for you to smile at him.

2. Thou shalt not say "sit still."

No one likes to sit still, not even adults. I've never heard anyone say, "Oh goodie, I get to sit still for a five-hour version of 'Hamlet!' And I can't wait for that ten-hour drive to Grandma's house next week! I love my desk job, because I get to sit still so much!'' So it stands to reason that your most successful pictures will be of moving kids. If you must have a still subject—say for a head shot, or a formal or group portrait—take frequent breaks to let the child move about in a constructive and controlled way. Don't let the kids tear around the studio. Join them in doing the hokey-pokey or making funny faces or even playing catch. After a breather like this, position the subject and continue to shoot.

3. **Thou shalt not try to make a child act or look like an adult.**

As I mentioned above, a child is a young person, not a miniature adult. Kids have shorter attention spans and different interests and capabilities from adults. Respect kids for who and what they are.

4. **Thou shalt not ask of a child anything thou would not ask of an adult.**

At a very early age, children develop a sense of themselves, a sense of dignity and decorum, and definite ideas about how they want to appear for the rest of the world. Just as you wouldn't insist an adult client wear a certain hat if she thinks it looks stupid, or jump, or go barefoot, neither should you insist a child do these things if it offends her sensibilities. You can ask, and if your suggestion is rebuffed, let it go. Sometimes after a while, the child will come back to your original suggestion and carry it out with glee as if she'd thought of it herself.

5. **Thou shalt have fun.**

If you are having fun, it's guaranteed that the child will, as well. You don't have to be a giggling idiot, but if you enjoy your work, the kids will know, and they'll be much more willing to cooperate.

6. **Thou shalt offer encouragement.**

Kids need you to tell them when they're great. When children like and trust you, they naturally want to please you, and the more pleased you are, the happier the child. *You have the greatest smile! What a super leap! What a fantastic elephant imitation.* But be sincere—kids can smell a phony a mile away.

7. **Thou shalt be generous.**

To make successful pictures of children, you must be generous in every way: your time, your film, your energy, your focus and attention—your very self. I book my child portrait clients at least an hour apart. If there are three or more kids per family, I allow an hour and a half to two hours. I shoot an average of thirty-six to seventy-two shots per kid. I have actually had parents ask me to provide fewer proofs, so there won't be so much to choose from. I go into every shooting day well rested and well exercised, knowing that I'm going to be jumping and laughing and expending just as much energy as my subjects.

I have been told by other photographers that they couldn't possibly afford to spend the time I do with each client or shoot as much film, or they would lose money. While it's true I make very little, if any, profit on the sitting itself, my print sales more than compensate for this. If your fee structure is such that it forces you to do a big volume of kids in a short amount of time to turn a profit, you won't have a very good success ratio. Maybe it's time for a change.

8. **Thou shalt not intimidate.**

Just because you're bigger than a kid and it's your studio doesn't mean you can or should be the boss. Forcefulness and intimidation may get you your own way, but it won't get you a great picture. Look at the making of the photo as a collaboration between equals—you and the child. Besides, anybody who has ever tried to get a child to eat his vegetables or wear his sweater knows that intimidation rarely works at any age. From the time we are infants we determine what goes in our mouths or on our bodies, and whether or not we stand in front of the camera and smile.

9. **Thou shalt not ingratiate.**

By the same token, never be ingratiating. You're still forcing yourself on the child, just in a different way. Relax and take the child's lead. She'll let you know how much she wants to let you into her personal space, and how quickly she can warm up to

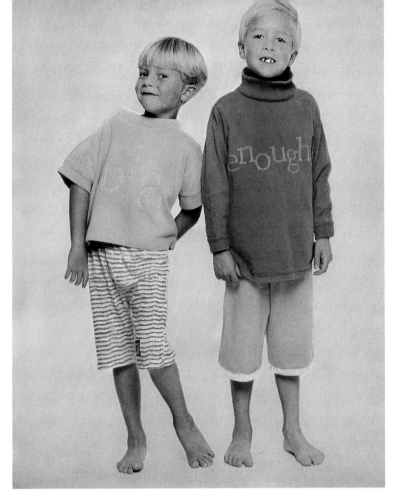

I gave the boy on the left a small ball just before I shot and asked him to hide it from the camera. You can't see the ball, but his resulting mischievous expression makes this a great portrait.

Strobe; studio; Nikon 8008; Nikkor 35-105mm zoom AF lens; Kodak Plus-X 100 (professional film); printed on Agfa Portriga 118 #2 contrast paper; hand-colored with Marshall photo oils and colored pencils.

you. All you have to do is be there and be ready when she is. I have a friend who is accomplished at both jazz and flamenco dancing. She explained the different attitudes inherent in these areas of dance. The jazz dancer goes out to the audience, and the flamenco dancer draws the audience in to herself. I suggest you be mindful of the flamenco dancer's lesson, and let the child come to you.

10. **Thou shalt embrace (controlled) chaos.**

We have only three rules in our studio—don't do anything that might hurt you; don't do anything that might hurt someone else; and don't do anything that might hurt the equipment. There's always a lot of jumping, running, shouting, music and antics going on at our studio. Parents who require a large amount of law and order often leave our studio looking frazzled. But there is a method to our madness—if we didn't have the (controlled) chaos, we wouldn't get the same level of spontaneity and naturalness. I find it's easier to calm an excited child down a bit than to light a fire under a sedate one.

Of course there are limits. If you let kids literally run wild, they reach a point where you simply can't calm and focus them again. So we control the chaos by directing the activity and taking part in it. We do the bunny hop, the hokeypokey, animal imitations, play catch, and more, in between and sometimes even during shooting.

Memorize these ten commandments, and you will be on your way to working successfully, and with a certain amount of ease, in photographing children. Numbers 5, 6, 7 and 8 will be a big help to you during the most critical phase of your interaction with your child subjects—the first five minutes.

While of course all children are individuals, and they all react to situations differently, there are certain behaviors one can predict with a certain amount of accuracy based on the child's age, placement within the family, and age difference between her and her siblings.

Babies (3 months to 1 year). The biggest problem with babies is that their inner clocks can change very quickly, so, if you book a shoot too far in advance, you're in danger of interfering with nap time, or lunch, or a plain old crabby mood. Encourage the parents to reschedule if it looks like the appointment is going to fall at a bad time. It'll just be a waste of everyone's time and energy if baby is tired, hungry, cutting a tooth, or not feeling well.

Toddlers (1 to 3 years). Toddlers can be unpredictable, too, because they are at an age when they're testing their boundaries, asserting their will, and discovering who they are. They are also highly mobile, and they like to move fast. Their moods are mercurial, and tears can be turned on and off like a faucet. The good news is that they almost never stay in a bad temper for long. The bad news is that their attention span is exactly one nanosecond. So allow plenty of time for the shoot to accommodate mood shifts, and refreshment and play breaks. Find ways to shoot them while they're moving and playing rather than trying to get them to sit. One method I've found useful is to set the child down at the far back corner of the backdrop and have his mother call to him from the front opposite corner. The child will run to his mother,

Approach the photo session as playtime, and you'll be rewarded with energetic, happy subjects like this one — and you'll have fun, too!

Strobe; Nikon 8008; 35-105mm zoom AF lens; Kodak Plus-X 100 (professional film); printed on Agfa Portriga 118 #2 contrast paper; sepia toned and hand-colored with Marshall photo oils and colored pencils.

usually laughing and smiling all the way, and Erik (my husband and partner) shoots when he's in the center of the drop.

Young children (3 to 5 years). This age group is a little quieter than the toddler group. They are old enough to reason with, and they usually want to please you. Their attention spans are a bit longer, and they start to have wild senses of humor.

Children (6 to 9 years). At this age you may experience the opposite problem from that of toddlers — *over*cooperation. You'll meet good little girls and boys who sit still and smile a little camera smile and do exactly as they are asked. You need to loosen them up and get them to forget themselves. It can work wonders to ask kids to teach you something: I've learned baseball pitches, knot tying, dog training, and all the names of the characters in *The Little Mermaid* from my 6- to 9-year-old friends.

Preteens (9 to 12 years). At this age kids can be charmingly awkward. They're part adult, part child, hauling their stuffed bear to the studio but also careful not to seem "babyish" or immature. Respect their sense of decorum, but don't lose your own sense of playfulness. Be open and accepting of both the child and the adult parts of them, but gently discourage any attempts at "cheesecake" or overly grown-up poses.

Teenagers (13 to 19 years). Teenagers need a lot of reassurance and they embarrass easily. Shower them with genuine compliments and encouragement — not just relating to their appearance, but to all their interests and abilities. Marvel at their athleticism, intelligence, hobbies and anything they'll share with you.

Only, oldest, middle and youngest children. Only children tend to be confident and gregarious. Oldest children try to be helpful — sometimes too helpful, as in overly controlling their younger siblings. Middle kids often need a little extra attention to shine. Youngest children are sometimes a little lazy, being used to having older siblings do things for them.

The new baby. Sometimes when there's a new baby in the family, older siblings try to get extra attention by regressing to baby-like behavior. If this happens, ignore the age-inappropriate behavior and ask the older child to help you meter the light, choose props, or hand you film. They'll get a kick out of getting attention for being big and capable while baby gets attention for being small.

Blended families. Frequently, siblings from different families of origin are spread apart in age, and this can make for some really fun pictures, with the younger ones crawling on and being tossed into the air by the older ones. In the studio, at least, blended families don't seem to have any more discord or to be any less happy than any other families.

**GETTING OFF
TO A GOOD
START**

The first five minutes you spend with the child will sometimes affect the entire shoot. To get off to a good start, introduce yourself, greet the child and make contact with him in a noninvasive way. Take the child's lead as to what kind of contact will be appropriate—some kids are immediately familiar, and they'll welcome you to kneel down at their level, make eye contact, shake their hands and chat. But for some kids, even this might feel too threatening. You'll have to let your intuition guide you. If you fault in one direction, let it be toward aloofness. Show a mild, genuine interest in the child, but don't be forced, falsely jolly or overly familiar.

Let the child know what to expect. Show him around the studio, show him the camera and where he'll be photographed, and tell him what you expect of him. Tell him you're going to play and have fun. Ask him a question to which he must answer yes. "Do you like juice? So do I. Apple is my favorite. Do you like to jump and play? So do I. And that's what we're going to do today." Ask him if there's anything in particular he'd like to do in the picture—frequently he'll already have a few ideas, and they'll probably be good ones. Agree on a few things before you start—that you'll do some baseball poses, some jumping shots, even one with a funny face or with his tongue sticking out. Use the first five minutes as a getting-to-know-you period.

PLAY AND TALK

After the first five minutes, the two most important words for a child photographer to remember are *play* and *talk*. A child's job is learning about her world, and she learns through play. When you play with her, you're helping her do her job.

Talking with children is the surest way to help them relax in front of the camera. Ask them questions about neighborhood kids, pets, school, hobbies, food—anything that interests them. Do some research: find out about Teenage Mutant Ninja Turtles; go to kids' movies; watch kids' TV. But also be careful—some parents don't allow their kids to watch cartoons they consider violent or to eat junk food. It's a good idea to find out in advance whether the child has ever eaten at McDonald's and if Winnie the Pooh is a better topic of conversation than Rambo.

I almost always find out about some of the child's interests from the parents when they book their photo shoot. Once I was in the middle of a delightful portrait session with a seven-year-old boy when I started to talk about the new hockey stick he'd gotten for his birthday and about the angel fish in his aquarium. Suddenly he looked ashen and refused to cooperate. Finally, he blurted, "How do you know all this stuff about me?" After I explained that his mother had told me about him, he was fine, but for a second there he feared I was some sort of omniscient oracle. Now I always precede any statement of knowledge about the child with, "Your mom tells me. . . ."

Use kids' names when you're directing them during a shoot. This is especially important when you're working with a group of three or more. Just saying, for instance, "Put your arm around your sister," may not attract the child's attention at all. But saying, "Ben, put your arm around Sarah," always gets results. This pyramid shot of four siblings could have quickly deteriorated into total chaos if I hadn't been able to direct all the kids by their names.

Strobe; studio; Nikon 8008; Nikkor 35-105mm AF lens; Kodak Plus-X 100 (professional film); printed on Agfa Portriga 118 #2 contrast paper; hand-colored with artist's oils and colored pencils.

When I first started working with kids, I asked around for ideas from other photographers, parents, social workers, day-care workers and others, on how to amuse and engage them. My queries were always met with vagueness. So when I decided to write this book, I vowed to offer concrete ways to interact that would help the photographer create expressive, natural pictures. Beyond simply talking and playing with kids, there are no magic tricks. But there are specific ways to talk and play that I've found encourage many kids to respond with genuine enthusiasm.

Storytelling. Some kids who are inhibited physically and don't want to jump or dance for the camera will open up and become unbelievably animated if you ask them to tell you a story, especially if you make one up together.

Catch. Catch is perhaps one of the best games in the world, enjoyed by children and adults. It not only relaxes your subjects and encourages dialogue, it also is one way of forging a connection. I play catch with kids, not only before and after the shoot, but during, too. I stand off camera and get a good volley going with the child. Meanwhile, Erik is getting some great pictures of the child holding out his hands to receive the ball, giggling, catching and winding up for the throw. Then I add an element to the game, saying, "Now after you throw the ball, look at the camera and jump! Now after you throw the ball, look at the camera and clap your hands!"

I've got your nose. Some kids really get a kick out of the old grandpa trick of grabbing at the nose, sticking your thumb between your fingers, and saying, "I've got your nose!" If you do this, be gentle, and always be ready to say, "Oh, it's okay, I don't really have your nose, see?" because some kids will believe you. You must admit, having a stranger walk off with your nose is a terrifying thought. Kids seem to have the most fun in getting your nose, rather than you getting their noses. They may grab your nose repeatedly. Be sure to pat your face and act surprised every time.

High fives and secret handshakes. Another way to form a connection with a child is to get him to give you a high five or teach him a secret handshake. It's another way of using play to establish common ground. The sillier the secret handshake, the better. Pinky wiggling, elbow bumping, and arm flapping are all excellent components. There's also the old game of, "Gimme five! Up high, down low . . . too slow!" in which you ask the child to slap your hand and then pull it away at the last second. This is also something that delights them to "trick" you back, again and again.

Hiding the ball. An uncooperative child from one to four years can be charmed if you give him a small ball and ask him to hide it from the camera. He'll hold it between his hands or behind his back, stuff it in his pocket or up his shirt, under his hat, or any number of surprising places, and then beam into the camera. Then pretend you don't know where it is and ask him to show it to you. When he procures it for you, act surprised and ask him to hide it again.

Reverse psychology. Sometimes if a child is being contrary, reverse psychology can work wonders. One four-year-old boy refused to stand on the seamless paper or to smile, instead stalking around the studio with a huge frown on his face. His quick-thinking father took off his own shoes and said, "Okay, guy, these are my shoes. Don't you dare put on my shoes." The boy immediately got a huge grin and made a beeline for his dad's shoes. "Oh no! Don't wear my shoes, and don't go onto the smiley face in them!" Dad cried in mock horror. Of course, the boy went right to his place on the seamless, wearing the shoes. "Oh my gosh! Get off of there right now! And whatever you do, don't smile!" cried the father. The boy giggled delightedly into the camera, and we got some great shots.

Peek-a-boo. Peek-a-boo can be lots of fun and can sometimes salvage a desperate situation. Ask the parent to put a hat, blanket, towel or other fabric over the child's head. Then say, "Gee, where did Dottie go? I don't see her." You'll probably hear giggling emanating from under the cover. The child will pull off the blanket and say, "Here I am!" "Wow, there she is. Where did you go?" The child will very likely put the cover back over her head and wait for more inquiries as to her whereabouts. Or have the parent hide behind the photographer, and say, "Where's your mommy?" Then have Mommy pop out, and then disappear again.

The penny press. If you're shooting a barefoot baby or toddler who won't stay within camera range or who simply isn't happy or is bored, you can sometimes elicit a smile or an interesting look by pressing an ordinary penny against the bottom of his foot. The penny will stick there for an instant, long enough for you to get out of the frame, and then when it falls off he'll bend over and pick it up, and then examine it, and eventually look into the camera.

Making funny faces. With small babies, making funny faces is one of the most natural and successful ways to connect. In my case, making funny faces is instinctive. If it's not for you, then practice in the mirror until you've built up a repertoire—it will be well worth the time.

Squeaky toys, rattles and noisemakers. Sometimes very young babies are too awed by new surroundings to focus on you or Mom or anything in the general direction of the camera. In these instances, when funny faces and dolls and puppets fail, I will use a squeaky toy or a rattle to get the baby to look toward the camera and smile.

Framing your requests. Sometimes your attitude in asking the child's cooperation makes the difference between success and failure. Instead of saying, "Susie, will you hold these flowers?" say, "Look, we get to play with these flowers now! Aren't they pretty? Do they smell good? How would you like to hold them?"

Kids do have definite ideas about what they do and don't want, but these ideas can change from moment to moment and situation to situation. Frequently they'll pick up on your attitude or their parents' attitudes when deciding what is or isn't fun. I recall one little girl who looked confused when I asked her what she wanted to wear in her picture. Finally she touched one dress and said, "Mommy, do I like wearing this?"

Narrow the field. It's important to give kids some control and some choices at the photo shoot, but too many choices can be overwhelming. So narrow down the options—instead of showing the child a pile of clothes and asking her to pick an outfit, show her two dresses and say, "Do you want to wear the pink one or the blue one?" Likewise with props, toys and poses. "Do you want to hold the bear or the fire truck? Do you want to jump or twirl?"

If Mom doesn't work, try Dad. Kids can be rather capricious about who they want to cooperate with at any given moment. More than a few two-year-olds have refused to wear hats or hold flowers proffered by their mom, but will gladly accept them from me. Or they won't wear a bow tied by me, but will wear one tied by Mom or Dad. So don't give up if one person fails to inspire cooperation. Try another—and another, until all the options are exhausted.

Bargaining. Sometimes bargaining works and sometimes it doesn't. Unbelievably precocious twenty-six-month-old Ronnie, who spoke in complete sentences, didn't

**Bear in mind that the clothes kids wear affect the mood
they project, their movement and expression. Compare
these shots of a two-year-old girl, the first in coveralls,
and the second in a dress. Though made within ten
minutes of each other, notice the different moods of
each shot.**

Strobe; studio; Nikon 8008; Nikkor 35-105mm zoom AF lens; Kodak Plus-X 100 (professional film); printed on Agfa Portriga 118
#2 contrast paper; hand-colored with Marshall photo oils and
colored pencils. Note that the shot on the right received the same
treatment as the shot on the left, but was sepia toned before
coloring.

want to wear her flip-up sunglasses. "Look, I have flip-ups too! I'll wear mine if you
wear yours," I said. Reluctantly she nodded. When I put mine on, and she still wouldn't
pick hers up off the floor, I said, "You said you'd wear yours if I wear mine." "No!"
"But we made a deal." "Then take yours off," she said. Her logic was indisputable.

Frequently a little bargaining can go a long way. "Three more in the glasses and
then you can hold your bear for some," usually evolves into ten or twenty shots as
the child has fun and forgets to count.

Bribes and rewards. Some kids will do anything for a Barbie doll or a McDonald's
hamburger. While the offer of bribes can be an effective way to elicit cooperation, I
never use it. If the parents want to offer a bribe or reward, that's fine, but I leave it
up to them. As a photographer, I have such a brief amount of time to spend with each
child that I feel it changes the relationship if I offer a payoff at the end of the session—
it implies somehow that the photo shoot is something to be tolerated, rather than
something that can be a reward in and of itself.

Mirroring. I discovered mirroring by accident when working with a five-year-old
girl. She obviously wanted to cooperate, but stood in a strangely adult, contemplative
pose and wouldn't move when I asked her to jump. "Come on, let's jump like a
bunny," I said, but she just stood with her hand on her chin and her legs crossed.
Suddenly it occurred to me that she was standing in exactly the same pose I was. So
I broke the pose and when I jumped, she jumped—I twirled, she twirled. You can
encourage the child to mirror your movements by subtly mirroring hers.

Secrets and secret words. Even the most uncooperative kids can't resist a secret. Sometimes if a child is restless, I whisper a secret word or phrase to him and
tell him to say it into the camera when I count to three. I do this ten or more times
in a row, changing the word each time. "Cowabunga" and "keep the change, you
filthy animal," are popular with the kids. Giving small kids words that are just a little
challenging to say can stimulate and amuse them—three-year-olds love to try to say
supercalafragilisticexpealidotious, and antidisestablishmentarianism. Lizard pizza and
boiled frogs work great, too.

If we're shooting siblings together I'll whisper a secret to one and have him whisper it to the other. While you sometimes get only a partial view of the whisperer's
face, the whisperee usually looks right into the camera, and this can result in an
excellent shot.

Shouting. Kids love to shout and they aren't allowed to do it very often. Especially when shooting a group of two or more, I ask them what their favorite food is, and then tell them to shout it out as loudly as they can. "What? I can't hear you," I shout back. We keep escalating, getting louder and louder, and the result is that in between shouts we get some really natural smiles.

Humor. I am convinced that kids have a sick sense of humor. But you don't have to resort to jokes involving bodily functions to get their attention. Ask them to tell you a joke—we all, adults included, laugh the hardest at our own jokes. I usually tell kids I need help coming up with jokes to tell other kids, and ask them if they have any that might work. They usually take this request for help very seriously and we can get a good shot of the child pondering his stock of jokes, followed by a big grin as he decides which one to tell. If you tell him a joke, speak a bit softly so he has to lean forward a little and concentrate to hear you.

I also sometimes resort to sight gags—a clown nose and Groucho glasses with a fake nose to elicit a giggle. Be careful not to try these with children who are too young, though, or you may have the opposite effect and frighten them.

Hitting yourself on the head with a rubber hammer can be good for a few yucks, especially if it squeaks.

Holding or balancing almost anything on your head is good for at least one good response shot. This is especially useful when I'm trying to talk a child out of holding a beloved object because it's too large and distracting, or it's appeared in enough pictures. I just say, "Your teddy bear is going to help me take your picture now," and then I put teddy on my head. Once that gets a chuckle, turn teddy upside down. Plead ignorance. "What's teddy doing up there now?" ask them. From there teddy might try to thump or eat my head. It's hard to master puppeteering and shooting simultaneously, but if you don't have a partner or an assistant, it's well worth the practice.

Instead of asking kids to say cheese, I ask them to say something silly, like, "It's not easy being cheesy," or, "Don't have a cow, man!" Sometimes even just the thought of saying one of these lines breaks them up and I get a good shot before they even say it.

Asking for help. Kids naturally want to please you, so if you invent ways in which they can help you, it makes the photo shoot more fun for them. I ask the kids to help by pushing the button on the light meter, watching or soothing younger siblings, and thinking up new, exciting games to play in front of the camera. Helping you out gives the child a chance to feel important and to feel that he has some control over the session.

Sometimes a child's first reaction to the photo studio is fear. Don't just assume you know what the child is afraid of—different kids may have very different fears. Ask what's scary. If the child isn't sure, or isn't old enough to verbalize it, let him pop the flash, look through the lens, see his mom or dad go first, and play with you on the backdrop for a while. Sometimes just discussing it helps.

Katie, a little two-year-old, came into our studio eager to have her picture taken (Mom had been pumping her up all week, telling her how much fun they would have, and telling her to say, "pho-to-grapher"), but when she got in front of the camera, she broke into tears with genuine fear. Thinking it would help if she left, Mom went for a walk in the hall while I asked Katie what was wrong.

Are you scared? A tearful nod.

What part is scary? A shrug.

Is it the flashing lights? No.

Is it the camera? No.

Is it Erik? To this, Katie looked at me sideways as if I were a bit slow and said, "No-o-o, silly."

Is it being all by yourself on that big backdrop with nobody near you? Pause. Voilà! Once we knew what the problem was, Mom came back into the studio and we spent some time playing sword fight with orchid branches on the backdrop. Gradually I moved out of the frame, then Mom did, and soon Katie was happily dancing, running and jumping for the camera. She even did her specialty—a little clenched jaw expression she called "hyperface."

While Katie was afraid of the isolation she felt all alone in the middle of the shooting bay, other children might be afraid of other things. A little exploration into the offending objects usually is all that's needed. If the child is afraid of the flashing strobes, I let her push the button and fire them off a few times. If she's afraid of the camera, I let her look through the lens at her mom, or even take a few shots of Mom herself.

Frequently a child's fear of a new activity can be diminished if she sees a familiar person doing it first. If the child doesn't want her picture taken, I'll take a few shots of the parents. I usually say, "Okay, Betsy, you stand over here by me and we're going to take some pictures of your mom and dad. Just your mom and dad alone, not with you, okay?" After about five seconds, most kids run to join their parents in front of the camera.

Even when you can't figure out exactly what the problem is, a play session on the backdrop, with or without Mom, is the best cure.

Given enough time and interaction, even children who come in hiding behind Mom's skirts will begin to enjoy the photo session and wind up saying, "Mom who?" It's natural for kids to have fun. But it's also natural for kids to experience some fear when faced with new and unfamiliar places and people. That fear will go away with some patience.

Some parents like to visit the studio a week or so before their scheduled shoot, to introduce the child to the surroundings and to me, and to watch another family shooting. While I welcome these preshoot visits, I don't find that they make any difference in the ultimate comfort of the child or the success of the photo session. These visits seem to be more valuable to the parent, to become acquainted with my personal style or to get ideas for what to bring along to their shoot.

USING MUSIC

When we shoot we almost always have a little music playing in the background. We generally keep it low so we don't have to strain to hear or be heard, unless the child requests it be turned up. We keep a collection of tapes that appeal to adults and older kids, as well as children's artists (Raffi seems to be the most popular).

OFFERING SNACKS

It's good to have some individual servings of a healthy, not-too-messy snack and some juice at your photo sessions. Keep the snacks out of sight and only offer them if the child's attention is growing short, or he needs a break or needs to be soothed. I stress individual portions because they help you limit the length of the snack break and the quantities consumed. I made the mistake of using jumbo packs of cookies and crackers in the fledgling months of Kidshooters, and sat and watched the clock tick as more than one small child refused to return to the photo session until he'd consumed twice his body weight in treats. With individual portions you can say, "all gone"—something even the youngest child understands. Raisins and bite-sized animal crackers are good selections. Avoid anything gooey, crumbly, chocolate or grape, or the child will probably wind up wearing most of it home.

THE WINDOW OF OPPORTUNITY The window of opportunity for great shots—the time when the studio and the photo session are comfortable enough so that the child isn't afraid, but new and interesting enough to amuse her—can seem pretty short sometimes. So try not to run behind schedule so you have to keep a family waiting. If you do, you'll probably be met with a bored, uncooperative kid and comments from the parents such as, "Well, she was smiling when we got here."

Of course, kids—like people of all ages—are individuals, and it's tough to make generalizations. Taken alone, none of these activities is a "sure thing." But they'll give you a place to begin, and then as you gain more and more experience in working with kids, you'll find ways to adapt these suggestions based on your own personality and sensibilities. If you find yourself at a loss, remember that you can always schedule a reshoot. But if you take the child's lead, treat her with respect, and maintain a spirit of playfulness, you can't help but succeed.

(Left.) Unlike babies, toddlers have a great range of movement. The challenge with this age group becomes getting them to stay on the backdrop.

Strobe; studio; Nikon 8008; Nikkor 35-105mm zoom AF lens; Kodak Plus-X 100 (professional film); printed on Agfa Portriga 118 #2 contrast paper; hand-colored with artist's oils and colored pencils.

(Right.) Teenagers follow instruction easily, and with encouragement make delightful subjects.

Strobe; studio; Nikon 8008; Nikkor 35-105mm zoom AF lens; Kodak Plus-X 100 (professional film); printed on Agfa Portriga 118 #2 contrast paper; hand-colored with artist's oils and colored pencils.

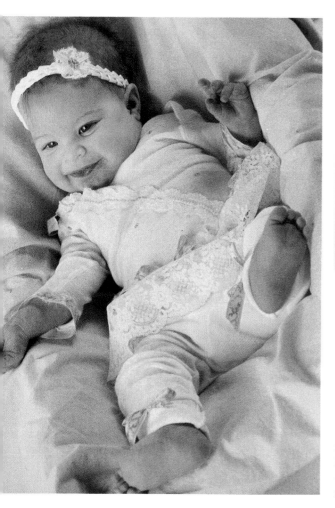

(Left.) Different childhood ages provide joys and challenges for the photographer. For example, if you catch a baby (up to 6 months) after a nap and a meal, she'll be a perfect subject, though she doesn't have much range of motion at that age.

Strobe; studio; Nikon 8008; Nikkor 35-105mm zoom AF lens; Kodak Plus-X 100 (professional film); printed on Agfa Portriga 118 #2 contrast paper; hand-colored with artist's oils and colored pencils.

Capturing the best expressions, attitudes and gestures is not a matter of "how," but "when." Rather than trying to contrive a pose, be ready to shoot when a great one comes naturally.

Strobes; studio; Nikon 8008; Nikkor 35-105mm zoom AF lens; Fuji Velvia 50.

When people see my work for the first time, they often ask me, "How did you get the children to 'pose' that way? They look so natural."

My response is that we didn't "get" them to do anything, and furthermore, there is no such thing as a pose. To pose implies stillness, and from the time we are born we are in perpetual motion. In my experience, the best photos are made, not when the child is "posed," or still, but when he is in movement from one attitude to another. It is not necessarily the moment of action, but the rising or descending from action that often makes the best picture.

My approach to shooting children is to simply capture the great expressions as they go by. It's much less a matter of "how" than of "when."

Genuine expressions of abandon are *absolutely fleeting*. Likewise, the right moment to capture them is when the child is in midair jumping, with her hair, arms and legs just so in the middle of twirling, or arms akimbo, dancing. No one can tell you when that perfect 250th of a second will occur, and you can't *know* when—you have to *feel* when. If you try to anticipate the action, you'll shoot too soon, and if you wait until you see something you like, by the time you press the button it'll be gone. So you have to learn to rely on your instinct and feelings. This may be difficult at first, when we seem to be taught in this culture to value thinking over feeling, judgment over intuition. You may be out of practice in trusting your instincts. But don't give up. Like so many other things, a cliché that we all learned in our own childhoods— practice makes perfect—proves true.

To snatch those in-between moments I sometimes ask a child to twirl around and then look into the camera. Shot at the moment she's about to twirl, or when she's recovering her orientation afterward, you see no evidence of the action of twirling at all, but you have a natural moment.

Often I ask a child to point her toe, look at her toe, then look into the camera. Putting together several simple motions can relax the child and help her to move naturally. I may shoot when she begins the action, in the middle, or after she's through, depending on how I feel.

CAPTURING

PEAK ACTION

OR EXPRESSION

The same principle of shooting during the in-between moments applies to capturing expressions as well as actions. I ask the child about his interests or to say something silly and shoot before he has a chance to speak. His reaction to my request is what I'm after. He doesn't have to say the phrase at all.

DON'T BE A STATUEMAKER When I was a child the neighborhood "gang" used to play a game called statuemaker. The kid designated as the statuemaker would grab the other kids by the arm one by one and spin them around until they were dizzy, then let go and shout, "Freeze!" The rest of the kids were obligated to freeze in whatever pose they were in when the leader shouted.

As a photographer, I try not to be a statuemaker. But there are times, for instance, if you're shooting a long exposure or with the child in very precise position, when you will have to ask your subjects to be very still.

If it's completely unavoidable, make a game out of it, and even the youngest kids can hold a pose, and, I'm pleased and surprised to say, even look natural doing it.

SETTING UP YOUR SHOT **Work fast.** Introduce the child to the setup at the very last possible moment and work as quickly as you can, without producing an atmosphere of urgency. If necessary, use a doll or other form approximately the same size and height as the child to set up the shot.

Quit while you're ahead. Most of the time my motto is, "Film is cheap!" I shoot as much as I can until I think I've captured what I need, and then some. But if a static

(Left.) These photos both have multiple subjects. Though they are positioned in a pleasing composition, they are not "posed" or still, but moving and natural.

Strobes; studio; Nikon 8008; Nikkor 35-105mm zoom AF lens; Kodak Plus-X (professional film); printed on Agfa Portriga 118 matte paper and hand-colored with Marshall photo oils and pencils, and artist's oils.

(Right.) Portraits with multiple subjects should portray not just each individual, but also the relationship between the subjects, as this playful shot of two sisters does.

Strobes; studio; Nikon 8008; Nikkor 35-105mm zoom AF lens; Kodak Plus-X (professional film); printed on Agfa Portriga 118 matte paper and hand-colored with Marshall photo oils and pencils, and artist's oils.

or controlled pose is needed, I find overwhelmingly that the first few shots of the take are by far the best, and the rest is often worthless. Don't belabor it, and run the risk of trying the child's patience. Get what you need, and stop. The first time I did this, I felt very insecure walking away from a photo session with only three shots. But with repeated success, I've learned to trust myself.

Use an assistant. If you're a professional photographer, enlist the help of the parent, or if you are the parent/photographer, enlist somebody to act as an assistant and sit as close to the child as possible (in the case of head shots, the helper can even be touching the child) and chat, play pat-a-cake, prompt, and generally amuse the child so that her attention doesn't wander and she doesn't feel isolated.

Plan a position that is as uncontrived and undemanding as possible. Have the subject sit down, stand or kneel. Anything that requires stamina, such as holding

(Above.) Photographing kids of different ages has its special joys and challenges. Toddlers, for instance, toddle, so it's easier and more natural to let them walk around and shoot as they go, rather than trying to get them to sit in one place.

Strobes; studio; Nikon 8008; Nikkor 35-105mm zoom AF lens; Fuji Velvia 50.

the arms up, is tough even for an adult to do for extended periods of time.

Do as I do. Demonstrate the position and expression you'd like to capture. Children are excellent mimics and eager to please. If you show them what you want, in addition to telling them, you'll be more likely to get it. Remember—a picture is worth a thousand words.

Avoid mug shots. Depending on what your goal is, you probably don't need to make pictures that are purely documental—what I call a mug shot. We've all seen them: child still, looking square into the camera, smiling, showing ears, eyes, teeth, tonsils and adenoids. A good portrait or portrait series can show little or none of the face, it can be a profile, it can even be a back view. One of my first forays into portrai-

(Left.) **Every picture needn't be all smiles. Quiet moments, and even tears, are all natural childhood expressions.**

Strobes; studio; Nikon 8008; Nikkor 35-105mm zoom AF lens; Fuji Velvia 50.

ture was at the age of fourteen. My sister was ten and very fond of a huge, wide-brimmed straw hat. The sight of her wearing the hat and walking away from me inspired me to pick up my Polaroid instant camera and shoot. The resulting photo is still a family favorite, even though it has long since faded.

At times you may be called on to make a purely documental picture of a kid: model's head shots, ID pictures, graduation and other school pictures — all require the subject to be represented more or less full-faced, and there is little room for expression either on the part of the subject or the photographer. But if you don't have to make mug shots, don't! If you have the drive to document and simply can't help yourself, try making a couple of mug shots at the beginning of each roll of film and forget it.

Shun perfection. One professional photographer who has spent his entire photographic career making wall-sized formal portraits always strove for "that one perfect pose" — shooting subject after subject frozen in classic poses with only the slightest variations. After reading an article about my studio, his comment was, "I can't wait to let them move!"

Posing children with their heads tipped or bowed over books, hands folded in their laps, ankles crossed, or in a number of other poses considered classic or traditional, may make a pretty (though predictable) composition, but they show nothing of the child's individual personality, nor do they portray the experience of childhood.

Strive for perfection and you'll miss capturing the exuberance, wonder, grace and explosive movements and expressions of childhood.

Beyond traditional poses, there is a whole realm of experience largely untapped by most portrait photographers. It is harder to categorize these, because they are not poses per se. So, I've divided them under different headings so that we can begin to explore them. Nontraditional and contemporary poses can be used successfully within all photographic genres, including portraiture.

NON-TRADITIONAL AND CONTEMPORARY POSES

Action poses include dancing, sports movements, leaping, twirling, playing air guitar, etc.

Natural poses are usually what we think of as candids: the child engrossed in play, lost in thought, examining a new object, hugging a familiar one, or simply talking and gesturing normally. Natural poses can be achieved at home, on location, or in the studio.

Retro poses mimic or partially re-create older styles of photographic poses of children that tended to either idealize children or make them appear to be tiny adults.

Don't strive for one "perfect" pose or your work will
lack spontaneity and vitality. Forget about that "wall-
sized" portrait and just try to capture the natural child.

Strobes; studio; Nikon 8008; Nikkor 35-105mm zoom AF lens;
Fuji Velvia 50.

The limitations of photographic technology frequently required the child to sit still for long exposures, sometimes held in place by hidden braces. For this reason I don't consider these true portraits. But poses reminiscent of these older styles can be charming and interesting, or even humorous, if executed tongue in cheek.

Stylized and editorial poses are used often by adult models in print and on the live runway, and more recently, in the new American dance form called "voguing." Kids often find this type of posing amusing and enjoy it as a game of pretend, allowing for some very natural expressions springing from this very unnatural style of movement.

WORKING WITH MULTIPLE SUBJECTS

Shooting multiple subjects is the most difficult to reconcile in terms of allowing the kids the freedom to move around, but still getting a shot that's also a good composition. I find it necessary to compromise by positioning my subjects. But once they are positioned I still encourage them to interact, gesture and express themselves freely. I don't always get everyone looking in the same direction, or everyone's full face in each shot, but the result is a picture that is better than a formally posed, static one.

When I shoot two siblings together I believe there are not just two subjects in the picture, but three: the two children and their relationship to one another. By formally posing the kids, you destroy any possibility of capturing that relationship. But if you position them leaving open all the possibilities for interaction and expression and movement, you can preserve amazing moments.

Take the picture of four siblings on page 124. The children are *positioned*—I asked the oldest boy to sit in the chair holding his baby sister, and the two middle children to stand on either side of the chair. That was all the instruction I gave them. The little girl naturally leaned in affectionately toward her nearest brother, the middle boy held the chair and regarded the camera nonchalantly, and the big brother comforted the baby, who was about to squirm off his lap. The mom of this quartet loves this shot, saying, "That's them, that's exactly how they are together. I've seen this scene in my living room a hundred times. I love it that you can tell that the baby is howling in tears in the next frame."

Of course, if all the kids had been posed, looking slightly off camera and smiling in the traditional way of formal portraits, the entire family relationship would have been absent from the shot.

It is certainly more difficult to make a good picture of a group of kids without posing them, but when you do, you capture the magic of portraying both the individual family and the universal experience of family.

My least favorite pose, and one, unfortunately, often used by portrait photographers, is the one in which the child is looking vaguely off to one side of the camera, because she is neither engaged in an activity nor with the camera (and hence, the viewer of the portrait). I believe the subject ideally should be either looking directly into the camera, or focusing her attention on something she is doing or holding.

Even though your subject is looking into the camera, this doesn't mean her expression, gestures and movement won't be natural. In fact, if you're carrying on a dialogue with her, it's only natural for her to look at you, hence, the camera. After a short time, most kids will forget the camera is there and will talk to it as if they are talking directly to me, without the lens in between. The camera needn't be hidden, and the child needn't seem unaware of the photographer to make a natural picture.

Many parents tell their kids at portrait sessions, "stop mugging!" But mugging, and trying out different expressions, is a natural part of childhood.

Strobes; studio; Nikon 8008; Nikkor 35-105mm zoom AF lens; Fuji Velvia 50.

**CAPTURING
MOVEMENT**
Of course, still, posed subjects are easier to photograph (where do you think we get the phrase, "sitting duck"?). But nothing worthwhile is easy, as any parent knows. It's tougher to make pictures of leaping, running, dancing kids. But movement can be captured using *quick, random shooting.*

Sometimes, if the child is exceptionally active or if he's performing a dance or a sports movement like pitching a baseball or ice skating, you can get good results by simply shooting quickly and randomly. This technique works best if you have a motor drive and an autofocus setting on your camera, but it can be accomplished without these features. Film is cheap, especially compared to a lost moment, so sometimes it's best to shoot a lot, even knowing that most of the shots won't be "keepers." That perfect picture, of a child at the moment her bat makes contact with the ball, or at the pinnacle of a graceful leap, is worth the seventy-two others that don't make the cut. However, don't make a habit of this kind of shooting. In most situations it's still best to make every shot deliberate. Other, more technique-oriented methods to capture movement are discussed in chapter 11.

To let kids feel relaxed and move naturally, they need the security to know that they're not all alone in front of the camera, and they need the freedom and space to move around, gesture and express themselves. By the same token, you the photographer need to be able to anticipate the child's movements and actions, and limit them to a degree to maintain control of his position in relationship to the lens, the field and your light source. Fortunately, there are methods that, used correctly, can give both you and the child what each of you needs.

SECURITY AND FREEDOM

Natural boundaries can keep a child in place without limiting his movement. In the studio, our lighting setup helps create a kind of cove, which I believe makes the child feel sheltered and at ease, and also keeps him naturally in the center of the drop. On location, finding areas that are partially enclosed can create a visually interesting field while giving the child a cozy niche to play in.

Anchors give subjects as much freedom of movement as possible, while still controlling their position in relation to the backdrop and the light sources. My anchor is simply a smiley face drawn on a drop. When I walk kids onto the drop, I point at the anchor and say, "There's your mark. You can jump and dance and do anything you want, so long as you stay near the smiley face." Even kids who are too little to take instruction are attracted to the tiny face, and we've gotten many excellent shots of one-year-olds pointing delightedly at the mark.

On location your anchor can be something as simple as a twig or a rock or a bald patch of grass—anything that won't read on film but which the child can see easily. Even if you're just shooting candids at home in the living room, a tiny piece of tape on the floor can work wonders for keeping your active subjects where you want them without restricting their movement too much.

Supports are useful for babies through toddlers, giving them something to pull themselves up or lean on. Supports should not overpower the child in the photo, but can help keep him in one place, and also have the added value of amusing him and helping him stay erect. Giant wooden toy blocks, rocking horses, child-sized chairs, and oversized stuffed animals are some anchors that can help lead to natural-looking baby and toddler "poses."

(Above.) We made this shot for a Christmas card whose legend read, ''Hats off to the Holidays!'' In order to get this cute expression and pose, we played a game of cowgirls, and the little girl is really yelling, ''Yee-hah!'' here.

Strobes; studio; Nikon 8008; Nikkor 35-105mm zoom AF lens; Kodak VPS III (professional film).

(Right.) By pretending to be a fairy, this girl created a graceful yet innocent dance, which we captured for a promotional postcard.

Strobes; studio; Nikon 8008; Nikkor 35-105mm zoom AF lens; Kodak Plus-X (professional film) printed on Agfa Portriga 118 matte paper and hand-colored with Marshall photo oils and pencils, and artist's oils.

**While I love action shots, a kid doesn't have to be jump-
ing or dancing to make a great portrait. Here is a series
of shots of two sisters, just "hanging out" and looking
natural.**

Strobes; studio; Nikon 8008; Nikkor 35-105mm zoom AF lens;
Kodak Plus-X (professional film); printed on Agfa Portriga 118
matte paper and hand-colored with Marshall photo oils and pencils, and artist's oils.

The child photographer must build a relationship with the parents as well as with their children, maintain a relaxed atmosphere during the shoot, and encourage good rapport between family members as well.

Strobes; studio; Nikon 8008; Nikkor 35-105mm zoom AF lens; Kodak Plus-X 100 (b&w professional film).

This final chapter will help professional child photographers appreciate the uniqueness of the people they really work for—the parents. And parents, this chapter will help you understand the inner workings of a photographer's mind.

KNOWLEDGE IS POWER

I always try to prepare the parents of my child clients for the shoot by giving them as much information as possible. Even if they've already seen examples of my work, I invite them to come to the studio, bring the kids, and watch another family's photo session. I tell them exactly what the various costs will be, so there is no room for surprise. I suggest tones and styles of clothing that work best for black-and-white and hand-colored pictures, as well as props and accessories. I give them explicit directions on how to get to the studio. When they schedule over the phone, I repeat the date and time of their appointment twice. When they book in person, I write the information on the back of my business card for them. Then, I send them a letter of confirmation stating everything all over again.

In addition to all the practical information, I try to give the parents a sense of who I am, and why I am a child photographer.

When I schedule an appointment I always prepare myself by getting the names and ages of the kids, and making notes about their special interests and hobbies. This serves a triple purpose: In chatting with the parents about their kids, I get to know them a little bit, and learn more about what they're looking for in a portrait; it puts the parents more at ease and improves their confidence in me as a portrait photographer and in my interest in their family; and it gives me a few tidbits to talk with the kids about at the photo session.

RULES FOR PARENTS

Just as you have rules for the kids to follow at the studio (no running, etc.), so should you have rules for the parents, too. But parents are not mind readers, so you have to tell them what is expected of them.

• How much do you want them to participate? Sometimes great expressions are elicited by mom and dad. Sometimes the kids are more comfortable and cooperative if mom and dad go for a walk in the hallway. Either way, spell it out.

• Some parents want to collaborate with you on the making of their child's portrait, acting like a sort of freelance art director. Some simply want the feeling of collaborating and are satisfied to be allowed to watch the proceedings and to have you offer an occasional explanation of what you're doing. My style of portraiture leaves a lot of room for input from the parents and the kids. You may or may not want a collaborator, so make it clear from the beginning whether you welcome their artistic input.

• Just as you adhere to Vik's Ten Commandments in chapter 10, so should you request that the parents do. No intimidating, no saying "Smile!" and no forcing performances. The child can be asked once to do his Roger Rabbit imitation or his Teenage Mutant Ninja Turtle trick, but he shouldn't be forced to do it, not even by a parent.

REMEMBER THE PERSONAL TOUCHES

Dale Carnegie was absolutely right: People like and trust you more when you remember their names and use them when you talk with them. I am blessed with an uncanny ability to remember the names of my clients, their kids, their pets and their kids' dolls. I'm able to surprise and flatter people when they call me a year after their photo session and say, "You probably don't remember me, but my name is Susie Doe . . ." and I say, "Oh, Jason's mom!" If your memory isn't that good, have a file for each family and write down all pertinent names in it.

Always voice an observation or make a sincere compliment to the parent about her child. Don't say, "Your kid is the most beautiful kid I've ever seen in my life!" The compliment needn't be appearance oriented. I rarely comment on kids' appearance because I believe there is already too much emphasis on looks in our culture as it is. Just say something that shows you're involved with, paying attention to, and *seeing* her child in a way that will allow you to make a successful portrait. "Gee, Donald is really into baseball," or, "It's nice how Trixie and Dixie get along so well together."

PHRASE BOOK OF PARENTESE

Sometimes you can feel like you need an interpreter to figure out what parents really mean when they say certain things. After years of experience, I've come up with this handy list of phrases for conversational parentese:

• **"Do you have kids yourself?"**

Translation: "What do you really know about kids and are you just in this for the money?"

• **"How did the pictures turn out?"**

Translation: "Did my kids perform adequately?" (I used to suspect this one really meant, "Did you have film in the camera, did the strobes fire, and did you expose the shots correctly?" I finally learned that it really means, "Did my kids perform adequately?")

• **"I have a six-month-old."**

Translation: "Can you retouch drool out of the pictures?"

• **"My baby just started walking."**

Translation: "Can you take a picture of a moving target?"

• **"I have a two-year-old."**

Translation: "Do you really think you can handle this?"

• **"I have a teenager."**

Translation: "My child is Doctor Jekyll and Mr. Hyde. She may cooperate with you or she may not, depending on her hormonal state. Do you think you can handle this?"

• **"My daughter likes to dress up."**

Translation: "I like my daughter to dress up."

Some parents are afraid we've never seen a baby cry, a two-year-old throw a temper tantrum, a six-year-old stick his tongue out, or a teenager behave sullenly. They need reassurance that their kids' quirks are all a part of the business—a part that you love—and that their kids are not the worst kids on the face of the earth. Sometimes parents seem to have a hard time being able to tell where they end and their child begins, so they feel as though they themselves are "misbehaving" when in fact their children are simply behaving like normal children.

BEYOND PHOTOGRAPHY

It's your job to see that any tension is eased, the session goes smoothly, no one wins or loses little tiffs, and you don't take sides. Practice selective blindness: you're cheerful, everything is going great, you don't notice any problems.

Treat the shoot like a big event. When you work five or more days a week in a photography studio you can become jaded to the fun and even glamorous aspects of your business. To us it may be a job, but to parents a photo session is an event. They probably bought special outfits for the kids, got them fresh haircuts, primed them to be "behaved," rearranged their schedules, and made a big effort to be there for their appointment and do what they could to make the shoot go well.

So you should make an effort to make the session fun, exciting and memorable. Remember that, while it can seem mundane to you, photography is still a glamorous business to most folks. That's why there's a cologne called Photo—do you think it smells like fixer? Capitalize on the glamour. Don't just give your clients a portrait; give them an experience.